The Pirates at Anchor.

Julius Cæsar

BY

JACOB ABBOTT

WITH ENGRAVINGS

NEW YORK AND LONDON

HARPER & BROTHERS PUBLISHERS

1901

PREFACE.

It is the object of this series of histories to present a clear, distinct, and connected narrative of the lives of those great personages who have in various ages of the world made themselves celebrated as leaders among mankind, and, by the part they have taken in the public affairs of great nations, have exerted the widest influence on the history of the human race. The end which the author has had in view is twofold: first, to communicate such information in respect to the subjects of his narratives as is important for the general reader to possess; and, secondly, to draw such moral lessons from the events described and the characters delineated as they may legitimately teach to the people of the present age. Though written in a direct and simple style, they are intended for, and addressed to, minds possessed of some considerable degree of maturity, for such minds only can fully appreciate the character and action which exhibits itself, as nearly all that is described in these volumes does, in close combination with the conduct and policy of governments, and the great events of international history.

CONTENTS.

ENGRAVINGS.

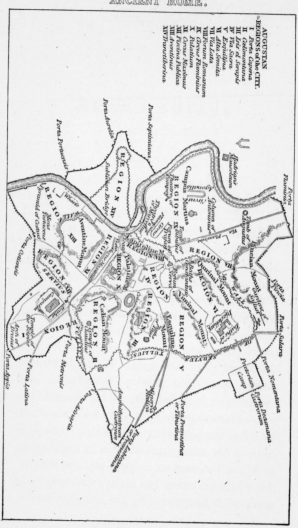

AUGUSTAN
REGIONS of the CITY.
I Porta Capena
II Cælimontana
III Isis et Serapis
IV Via Sacra
V Esquilina
VI Alta Semita
VII Via Lata
VIII Forum Romanum
IX Circus Flaminius
X Palatium
XI Circus Maximus
XII Piscina Publica
XIII Aventinus
XIV Transtiberina

JULIUS CÆSAR.

CHAPTER I.
MARIUS AND SYLLA.

THERE were three great European nations in ancient days, each of which furnished history with a hero: the Greeks, the Carthaginians, and the Romans.

Alexander was the hero of the Greeks. He was King of Macedon, a country lying north of Greece proper. He headed an army of his countrymen, and made an excursion for conquest and glory into Asia He made himself master of all that quarter of the globe, and reigned over it in Babylon, till he brought himself to an early grave by the excesses into which his boundless prosperity allured him. His fame rests on his triumphant success in building up for himself so vast an empire, and the admiration which his career has always excited among mankind is heightened by the consideration of

his youth, and of the noble and generous im
pulses which strongly marked his character.

The Carthaginian hero was Hannibal. We
class the Carthaginians among the European
nations of antiquity; for, in respect to their origin, their civilization, and all their commercial
and political relations, they belonged to the European race, though it is true that their capital
was on the African side of the Mediterranean
Sea. Hannibal was the great Carthaginian
hero. He earned his fame by the energy and
implacableness of his hate. The work of his
life was to keep a vast empire in a state of con-
tinual anxiety and terror for fifty years, so that
his claim to greatness and glory rests on the determination, the perseverance, and the success
with which he fulfilled his function of being,
while he lived, the terror of the world.

The Roman hero was Cæsar. He was born
just one hundred years before the Christian era.
His renown does not depend, like that of Alexander, on foreign conquests, nor, like that of Hannibal, on the terrible energy of his aggressions
upon foreign foes, but upon his protracted and
dreadful contests with, and ultimate triumphs
over, his rivals and competitors at home When
he appeared upon the stage, the Roman empire

already included nearly all of the world that
was worth possessing. There were no more
conquests to be made. Cæsar did, indeed, en-
large, in some degree, the boundaries of the empire; but the main question in his day was,
who should possess the power which preceding
conquerors had acquired.

The Roman empire, as it existed in those
days, must not be conceived of by the reader
as united together under one compact and con-
solidated government. It was, on the other
hand, a vast congeries of nations, widely dissim-
ilar in every respect from each other, speaking
various languages, and having various customs
and laws. They were all, however, more or
less dependent upon, and connected with, the
great central power. Some of these countries
were provinces, and were governed by officers
appointed and sent out by the authorities at
Rome. These governors had to collect the taxes of their provinces, and also to preside over
and direct, in many important respects, the administration of justice. They had, accordingly, abundant opportunities to enrich themselves
while thus in office, by collecting more money
than they paid over to the government at home,
and by taking bribes to favor the rich man's

cause in court. Thus the more wealthy and prosperous provinces were objects of great competition among aspirants for office at Rome. Leading men would get these appointments, and, after remaining long enough in their provinces to acquire a fortune, would come back to Rome, and expend it in intrigues and maneuvers to obtain higher offices still.

Whenever there was any foreign war to be carried on with a distant nation or tribe, there was always a great eagerness among all the military officers of the state to be appointed to the command. They each felt sure that they should conquer in the contest, and they could enrich themselves still more rapidly by the spoils of victory in war, than by extortion and bribes in the government of a province in peace. Then, besides, a victorious general coming back to Rome always found that his military renown added vastly to his influence and power in the city. He was welcomed with celebrations and triumphs; the people flocked to see him and to shout his praise. He placed his trophies of victory in the temples, and entertained the populace with games and shows, and with combats of gladiators or of wild beasts, which he had brought home with him for this purpose in the

train of his army. While he was thus enjoying his triumph, his political enemies would be
thrown into the back ground and into the shade;
unless, indeed, some one of them might himself
be earning the same honors in some other field,
to come back in due time, and claim his share
of power and celebrity in his turn. In this case,
Rome would be sometimes distracted and rent
by the conflicts and contentions of military rivals, who had acquired powers too vast for all
the civil influences of the Republic to regulate
or control.

There had been two such rivals just before
the time of Cæsar, who had filled the world with
their quarrels. They were Marius and Sylla.
Their very names have been, in all ages of the
world, since their day, the symbols of rivalry
and hate. They were the representatives re-
spectively of the two great parties into which
the Roman state, like every other community
in which the population at large have any voice
in governing, always has been, and probably always will be divided, the upper and the lower;
or, as they were called in those days, the patrician and the plebeian. Sylla was the patrician;
the higher and more aristocratic portions of the
community were on his side. Marius was the

favorite of the plebeian masses. In the contests,
however, which they waged with each other,

ROMAN PLEBEIANS.

they did not trust to the mere influence of votes.
They relied much more upon the soldiers they
could gather under their respective standards,
and upon their power of intimidating, by means
of them, the Roman assemblies. There was a

war to be waged with Mithridates, a very powerful Asiatic monarch, which promised great opportunities for acquiring fame and plunder.
Sylla was appointed to the command. While
he was absent, however, upon some campaign
in Italy, Marius contrived to have the decision
reversed, and the command transferred to him
Two officers, called tribunes, were sent to Syl
la's camp to inform him of the change. Sylla
killed the officers for daring to bring him such
a message, and began immediately to march toward Rome. In retaliation for the murder of
the tribunes, the party of Marius in the city
killed some of Sylla's prominent friends there,
and a general alarm spread itself throughout
the population. The Senate, which was a sort
of House of Lords, embodying mainly the power and influence of the patrician party, and was,
of course, on Sylla's side, sent out to him, when
he had arrived within a few miles of the city,
urging him to come no further. He pretended
to comply; he marked out the ground for a
camp; but he did not, on that account, materially delay his march. The next morning he
was in possession of the city. The friends of
Marius attempted to resist him, by throwing
stones upon his troops from the roofs of the

houses. Sylla ordered every house from which these symptoms of resistance appeared to be set on fire. Thus the whole population of a vast and wealthy city were thrown into a condition of extreme danger and terror, by the conflicts of two great bands of armed men, each claiming to be their friends.

Marius was conquered in this struggle, and fled for his life. Many of the friends whom he left behind him were killed. The Senate were assembled, and, at Sylla's orders, a decree was passed declaring Marius a public enemy, and offering a reward to any one who would bring his head back to Rome.

Marius fled, friendless and alone, to the southward, hunted every where by men who were eager to get the reward offered for his head. After various romantic adventures and narrow escapes, he succeeded in making his way across the Mediterranean Sea, and found at last a refuge in a hut among the ruins of Carthage. He was an old man, being now over seventy years of age.

Of course, Sylla thought that his great rival and enemy was now finally disposed of, and he accordingly began to make preparations for his Asiatic campaign. He raised his army, built

and equipped a fleet, and went away. As soon
as he was gone, Marius's friends in the city began to come forth, and to take measures for re-
instating themselves in power. Marius returned, too, from Africa, and soon gathered about
him a large army. Being the friend, as he pretended, of the lower classes of society, he collected vast multitudes of revolted slaves, out-
laws, and other desperadoes, and advanced toward Rome. He assumed, himself, the dress,
and air, and savage demeanor of his followers.
His countenance had been rendered haggard
and cadaverous partly by the influence of exposures, hardships, and suffering upon his advanced age, and partly by the stern and moody
plans and determinations of revenge which his
mind was perpetually revolving. He listened
to the deputations which the Roman Senate sent
out to him from time to time, as he advanced
toward the city, but refused to make any terms.
He moved forward with all the outward deliberation and calmness suitable to his years, while
all the ferocity of a tiger was burning within.

As soon as he had gained possession of the
city, he began his work of destruction. He first
beheaded one of the consuls, and ordered his
head to be set up, as a public spectacle, in the

22   JULIUS CÆSAR.   [B.C. 100.

Executions by order of Marius.   The Tarpeian Rock.

most conspicuous place in the city. This was
the beginning. All the prominent friends of
Sylla, men of the highest rank and station,
were then killed, wherever they could be found,
without sentence, without trial, without any
other accusation, even, than the military decision of Marius that they were his enemies, and
must die. For those against whom he felt any
special animosity, he contrived some special
mode of execution. One, whose fate he wished particularly to signalize, was thrown down
from the Tarpeian Rock.

The Tarpeian Rock was a precipice about
fifty feet high, which is still to be seen in Rome,
from which the worst of state criminals were
sometimes thrown. They were taken up to the
top by a stair, and were then hurled from the
summit, to die miserably, writhing in agony after their fall, upon the rocks below.

The Tarpeian Rock received its name from
the ancient story of Tarpeia. The tale is, that
Tarpeia was a Roman girl, who lived at a time
in the earliest periods of the Roman history,
when the city was besieged by an army from
one of the neighboring nations. Besides their
shields, the story is that the soldiers had gold-
en bracelets upon their arms They wished

Tarpeia to open the gates and let them in. She promised to do so if they would give her their bracelets; but, as she did not know the name of the shining ornaments, the language she used to designate them was, "Those things you have upon your arms." The soldiers acceded to her terms; she opened the gates, and they, instead of giving her the bracelets, threw their *shields* upon her as they passed, until the poor girl was crushed down with them and destroyed. This was near the Tarpeian Rock, which afterward took her name. The rock is now found to be perforated by a great many subterranean passages, the remains, probably, of ancient quarries. Some of these galleries are now walled up; others are open; and the people who live around the spot believe, it is said, to this day, that Tarpeia herself sits, enchanted, far in the interior of these caverns, covered with gold and jewels, but that whoever attempts to find her is fated by an irresistible destiny to lose his way, and he never returns. The last story is probably as true as the other.

Marius continued his executions and massacres until the whole of Sylla's party had been slain or put to flight. He made every effort to discover Sylla's wife and child, with a view to destroying them also, but they could not be found. Some friends of Sylla, taking compassion on their innocence and helplessness, concealed them, and thus saved Marius from the commission of one intended crime. Marius was disappointed, too, in some other cases, where men whom he had intended to kill destroyed themselves to baffle his vengeance. One shut himself up in a room with burning charcoal, and was suffocated with the fumes. Another bled himself to death upon a public altar, calling down the judgments of the god to whom he offered this dreadful sacrifice, upon the head of the tyrant whose atrocious cruelty he was thus attempting to evade.

By the time that Marius had got fairly established in his new position, and was completely master of Rome, and the city had begun to recover a little from the shock and consternation produced by his executions, he fell sick. He was attacked with an acute disease of great violence. The attack was perhaps produced, and was certainly aggravated by, the great mental excitements through which he had passed during his exile, and in the entire change of fortune which had attended his re-

turn. From being a wretched fugitive, hiding
for his life among gloomy and desolate ruins,
he found himself suddenly transferred to the
mastery of the world. His mind was excited,
too, in respect to Sylla, whom he had not yet
reached or subdued, but who was still prosecu-
ting his war against Mithridates. Marius had
had him pronounced by the Senate an enemy to
his country, and was meditating plans to reach
him in his distant province, considering his triumph incomplete as long as his great rival was
at liberty and alive. The sickness cut short
these plans, but it only inflamed to double violence the excitement and the agitations which
attended them.

As the dying tyrant tossed restlessly upon
his bed, it was plain that the delirious ravings
which he began soon to utter were excited by
the same sentiments of insatiable ambition and
ferocious hate whose calmer dictates he had
obeyed when well. He imagined that he had
succeeded in supplanting Sylla in his command,
and that he was himself in Asia at the head of
his armies. Impressed with this idea, he stared
wildly around; he called aloud the name of Mithridates; he shouted orders to imaginary troops;
he struggled to break away from the restraints

which the attendants about his bedside imposed, to attack the phantom foes which haunted
him in his dreams. This continued for several
days, and when at last nature was exhausted
by the violence of these paroxysms of phrensy,
the vital powers which had be 1 for seventy long
years spending their strength in deeds of self-
ishness, cruelty, and hatred, found their work
done, and sunk to revive no more.

Marius left a son, of the same name with him
self, who attempted to retain his father's power; but Sylla, having brought his war with
Mithridates to a conclusion, was now on his return from Asia, and it was very evident that a
terrible conflict was about to ensue. Sylla advanced triumphantly through the country, while
Marius the younger and his partisans concentrated their forces about the city, and prepared
for defense. The people of the city were divided, the aristocratic faction adhering to the
cause of Sylla, while the democratic influences
a ded with Marius. Political parties rise and
fall, in almost all ages of the world, in alternate
fluctuations, like those of the tides. The faction of Marius had been for some time in the
ascendency, and it was now its turn to fall.
Sylla found, therefore, as he advanced, every

thing favorable to the restoration of his own party to power. He destroyed the armies which came out to oppose him. He shut up the young Marius in a city not far from Rome, where he had endeavored to find shelter and protection, and then advanced himself and took possession of the city. There he caused to be enacted again the horrid scenes of massacre and murder which Marius had perpetrated before, going, however, as much beyond the example which he followed as men usually do in the commission of crime. He gave out lists of the names of men whom he wished to have destroyed, and these unhappy victims of his revenge were to be hunted out by bands of reckless soldiers, in their dwellings, or in the places of public resort in the city, and dispatched by the sword wherever they could be found. The scenes which these deeds created in a vast and populous city can scarcely be conceived of by those who have never witnessed the horrors produced by the massacres of civil war. Sylla himself went through with this work in the most cool and unconcerned manner, as if he were performing the most ordinary duties of an officer of state He called the Senate together one day, and, while he was addressing them, the attention of

the Assembly was suddenly distracted by the
noise of outcries and screams in the neighboring streets from those who were suffering military execution there.   The senators started
with horror at the sound.   Sylla, with an air
of great composure and unconcern, directed the
members to listen to him, and to pay no attention to what was passing elsewhere.   The
sounds that they heard were, he said, only
some correction which was bestowed by his orders on certain disturbers of the public peace.

Sylla's orders for the execution of those who
had taken an active part against him were not
confined to Rome.   They went to the neighboring cities and to distant provinces, carrying
terror and distress every where.   Still, dreadful as these evils were, it is possible for us, in
the conceptions which we form, to overrate the
extent of them.   In reading the history of the
Roman empire during the civil wars of Marius and Sylla, one might easily imagine that
the whole population of the country was organ
zed into the two contending armies, and were
employed wholly in the work of fighting with
and massacring each other.   But nothing like
this can be true.   It is obviously but a small
part, after all, of an extended community that

can be ever actively and personally engaged in
these deeds of violence and blood.   Man is not
naturally a ferocious wild beast.   On the contrary, he loves, ordinarily, to live in peace and
quietness, to till his lands and tend his flocks,
and to enjoy the blessings of peace and repose.
It is comparatively but a small number in any
age of the world, and in any nation, whose passions of ambition, hatred, or revenge become
so strong as that they love bloodshed and war.
But these few, when they once get weapons
into their hands, trample recklessly and mercilessly upon the rest.   One ferocious human tiger, with a spear or a bayonet to brandish, will
tyrannize as he pleases over a hundred quiet
men, who are armed only with shepherds'
crooks, and whose only desire is to live in
peace with their wives and their children.

Thus, while Marius and Sylla, with some
hundred thousand armed and reckless followers,
were carrying terror and dismay wherever they
went, there were many millions of herdsmen
and husbandmen in the Roman world who were
dwelling in all the peace and quietness they
could command, improving with their peaceful
industry every acre where corn would ripen or
grass grow.   It was by taxing and plundering

the proceeds of this industry that the generals
and soldiers, the consuls and prætors, and pro
consuls and proprætors, filled their treasuries,
and fed their troops, and paid the artisans for
fabricating their arms.   With these avails they
built the magnificent edifices of Rome, and
adorned its environs with sumptuous villas.
As they had the power and the arms in their
hands, the peaceful and the industrious had no
alternative but to submit.   They went on as
well as they could with their labors, bearing
patiently every interruption, returning again
to till their fields after the desolating march of
the army had passed away, and repairing the
injuries of violence, and the losses sustained by
plunder, without useless repining.   They looked upon an armed government as a necessary
and inevitable affliction of humanity, and submitted to its destructive violence as they would
submit to an earthquake or a pestilence.   The
tillers of the soil manage better in this country
at the present day.   They have the power in
their own hands, and they watch very narrow-
ly to prevent the organization of such hordes
of armed desperadoes as have held the peaceful
inhabitants of Europe in terror from the earliest periods down to the present day.

When Sylla returned to Rome, and took possession of the supreme power there, in looking over the lists of public men, there was one whom he did not know at first what to do with. It was the young Julius Cæsar, the subject of this history. Cæsar was, by birth, patrician, having descended from a long line of noble ancestors. There had been, before his day, a great many Cæsars who had held the highest offices of the state, and many of them had been celebrated in history. He naturally, therefore, belonged to Sylla's side, as Sylla was the representative of the patrician interest. But then Cæsar had personally been inclined toward the party of Marius. The elder Marius had married his aunt, and, besides, Cæsar himself had married the daughter of Cinna, who had been the most efficient and powerful of Marius's coadjutors and friends. Cæsar was at this time a very young man, and he was of an ardent and reckless character, though he had, thus far, taken no active part in public affairs. Sylla overlooked him for a time, but at length was about to put his name on the list of the proscribed. Some of the nobles, who were friends both of Sylla and of Cæsar too, interceded for the young man; Sylla yielded to their request, or, rather, suspended his decision, and sent orders to Cæsar to repudiate his wife, the daughter of Cinna. Her name was Cornelia. Cæsar absolutely refused to repudiate his wife. He was influenced in this decision partly by affection for Cornelia, and partly by a sort of stern and indomitable insubmissiveness, which formed, from his earliest years, a prominent trait in his character, and which led him, during all his life, to brave every possible danger rather than allow himself to be controlled. Cæsar knew very well that, when this his refusal should be reported to Sylla, the next order would be for his destruction. He accordingly fled. Sylla deprived him of his titles and offices, confiscated his wife's fortune and his own patrimonial estate, and put his name upon the list of the public enemies. Thus Cæsar became a fugitive and an exile. The adventures which befell him in his wanderings will be described in the following chapter

Sylla was now in the possession of absolute power. He was master of Rome, and of all the countries over which Rome held sway. Still he was nominally not a magistrate, but only a general returning victoriously from his Asiatic campaign, and putting to death, somewhat irregularly, it is true, by a sort of martial law.

persons whom he found, as he said, disturbing
the public peace. After having thus effectually
disposed of the power of his enemies, he laid
aside, ostensibly, the government of the sword,
and submitted himself and his future measures
to the control of law. He placed himself ostensibly at the disposition of the city. They
chose him dictator, which was investing him
with absolute and unlimited power. He remained on this, the highest pinnacle of worldly
ambition, a short time, and then resigned his
power, and devoted the remainder of his days to
literary pursuits and pleasures. Monster as he
was in the cruelties which he inflicted upon his
political foes, he was intellectually of a refined
and cultivated mind, and felt an ardent interest
in the promotion of literature and the arts.

The quarrel between Marius and Sylla, in
respect to every thing which can make such a
contest great, stands in the estimation of mankind as the greatest personal quarrel which the
history of the world has ever recorded. Its
origin was in the simple personal rivalry of
two ambitious men. It involved, in its consequences, the peace and happiness of the world.
In their reckless struggles, the fierce combatants
trampled on every thing that came in their way,

and destroyed mercilessly, each in his turn, all
that opposed them.   Mankind have always ex-
ecrated their crimes, but have never ceased to
admire the frightful and almost superhuman
energy with which they committed them.

CHAPTER II.

CÆSAR'S EARLY YEARS.

CÆSAR does not seem to have been much disheartened and depressed by his misfortunes. He possessed in his early life more than the usual share of buoyancy and light-heartedness of youth, and he went away from Rome to enter, perhaps, upon years of exile and wandering, with a determination to face boldly and to brave the evils and dangers which surrounded him, and not to succumb to them.

Sometimes they who become great in their maturer years are thoughtful, grave, and sedate when young. It was not so, however, with Cæsar. He was of a very gay and lively disposition. He was tall and handsome in his person, fascinating in his manners, and fond of society, as people always are who know or who suppose that they shine in it. He had seemed, in a word, during his residence at Rome, wholly intent upon the pleasures of a gay and joyous life, and upon the personal observation which his rank, his wealth, his agreeable manners

and his position in society secured for him. In
fact, they who observed and studied his character in these early years, thought that, although
his situation was very favorable for acquiring
power and renown, he would never feel any
strong degree of ambition to avail himself of its
advantages. He was too much interested, they
thought, in personal pleasures ever to become
great, either as a military commander or a
statesman.

Sylla, however, thought differently. He had
penetration enough to perceive, beneath all the
gayety and love of pleasure which characterized
Cæsar's youthful life, the germs of a sterner
and more aspiring spirit, which, he was very
sorry to see, was likely to expend its future
energies in hostility to him. By refusing to
submit to Sylla's commands, Cæsar had, in effect, thrown himself entirely upon the other
party, and would be, of course, in future iden-
tified with them. Sylla consequently looked
upon him now as a confirmed and settled enemy. Some friends of Cæsar among the patrician families interceded in his behalf with Sylla again, after he had fled from Rome. They
wished Sylla to pardon him, saying that he was
a mere boy and could do him no harm. Sylla

shook his head, saying that, young as he was, he saw in him indications of a future power which he thought was more to be dreaded than that of many Mariuses.

One reason which led Sylla to form this opinion of Cæsar was, that the young nobleman, with all his love of gayety and pleasure, had not neglected his studies, but had taken great pains to perfect himself in such intellectual pursuits as ambitious men who looked forward to political influence and ascendency were accustomed to prosecute in those days He had studied the Greek language, and read the works of Greek historians; and he attended lectures on philosophy and rhetoric, and was obviously interested deeply in acquiring power as a public speaker. To write and speak well gave a public man great influence in those days. Many of the measures of the government were determined by the action of great assemblies of the free citizens, which action was itself, in a great measure, controlled by the harangues of orators who had such powers of voice and such qualities of mind as enabled them to gain the attention and sway the opinions of large bodies of men.

It must not be supposed, however, that this

popular power was shared by all the inhabitants of the city. At one time, when the population of the city was about three millions the
number of free citizens was only three hundred
thousand. The rest were laborers, artisans,
and slaves, who had no voice in public affairs.
The free citizens held very frequent public assemblies. There were various squares and open
spaces in the city where such assemblies were
convened, and where courts of justice were held.
The Roman name for such a square was *forum*.
There was one which was distinguished above
all the rest, and was called emphatically The
Forum. It was a magnificent square, surrounded by splendid edifices, and ornamented by
sculptures and statues without number. There
were ranges of porticoes along the sides, where
the people were sheltered from the weather
when necessary, though it is seldom that there
is any necessity for shelter under an Italian
sky   In this area and under these porticoes
the people held their assemblies, and here courts
of justice were accustomed to sit. The Forum
was ornamented continually with new monuments, temples, statues, and columns by successful generals returning in triumph from foreign campaigns, and by proconsuls and prætors

A ROMAN FORUM

coming back enriched from their provinces, until it was fairly choked up with its architectural magnificence, and it had at last to be partially cleared again, as one would thin out too dense a forest, in order to make room for the assemblies which it was its main function to contain.

The people of Rome had, of course, no printed books, and yet they were mentally cultivated and refined, and were qualified for a very high appreciation of intellectual pursuits and pleasures. In the absence, therefore, of all facilities for private reading, the Forum became the great central point of attraction. The same kind of interest which, in our day, finds its gratification in reading volumes of printed history quietly at home, or in silently perusing the columns of newspapers and magazines in libraries and reading-rooms, where a whisper is seldom heard, in Cæsar's day brought every body to the Forum, to listen to historical harangues, or political discussions, or forensic arguments in the midst of noisy crowds. Here all tidings centered; here all questions were discussed and all great elections held. Here were waged those ceaseless conflicts of ambition and struggles of power on which the fate of nations, and sometimes the

welfare of almost half mankind depended. Of
course, every ambitious man who aspired to an
ascendency over his fellow-men, wished to make
his voice heard in the Forum. To calm the
boisterous tumult there, and to hold, as some
of the Roman orators could do, the vast assemblies in silent and breathless attention, was a
power as delightful in its exercise as it was glorious in its fame. Cæsar had felt this ambition,
and had devoted himself very earnestly to the
study of oratory.

His teacher was Apollonius, a philosopher and
rhetorician from Rhodes. Rhodes is a Grecian
island, near the southwestern coast of Asia Minor. Apollonius was a teacher of great celebrity, and Cæsar became a very able writer and
speaker under his instructions. His time and
attention were, in fact, strangely divided between the highest and noblest intellectual avocations, and the lowest sensual pleasures of a
gay and dissipated life. The coming of Sylla
had, however, interrupted all ; and, after receiving the dictator's command to give up his
wife and abandon the Marian faction, and de-
termining to disobey it, he fled suddenly from
Rome, as was stated at the close of the last
chapter, at midnight, and in disguise.

He was sick, too, at the time, with an inter
mittent fever.   The paroxysm returned once in
three or four days, leaving him in tolerable
health during the interval.   He went first into
the country of the Sabines, northeast of Rome,
where he wandered up and down, exposed continually to great dangers from those who knew
that he was an object of the great dictator's displeasure, and who were sure of favor and of a
reward if they could carry his head to Sylla
He had to change his quarters every day, and
to resort to every possible mode of concealment.
He was, however, at last discovered, and seized
by a centurion.   A centurion was a commander
of a hundred men; his rank and his position
therefore, corresponded somewhat with those of
a *captain* in a modern army.   Cæsar was not
much disturbed at this accident.   He offered
the centurion a bribe sufficient to induce him
to give up his prisoner, and so escaped.

The two ancient historians, whose records
contain nearly all the particulars of the early
life of Cæsar which are now known, give somewhat contradictory accounts of the adventures
which befell him during his subsequent wanderings.   They relate, in general, the same incidents, but in such different connections, that the

14   J U L *i* U S   C Æ S A R   ¸B.C. 80–70

Cæsar in Asia Minor.   He joins the court of Nicomedes

precise chronological order of the events which
occurred can not now be ascertained. At all
events, Cæsar, finding that he was no longer safe
in the vicinity of Rome, moved gradually to the
eastward, attended by a few followers, until he
reached the sea, and there he embarked on
board a ship to leave his native land altogether
After various adventures and wanderings, he
found himself at length in Asia Minor, and he
made his way at last to the kingdom of Bithynia, on the northern shore. The name of the
king of Bithynia was Nicomedes. Cæsar joined
himself to Nicomedes's court, and entered into
his service. In the mean time, Sylla had ceased
to pursue him, and ultimately granted him a
pardon, but whether before or after this time is
not now to be ascertained. At all events, Cæsar
became interested in the scenes and enjoyments
of Nicomedes's court, and allowed the time to
pass away without forming any plans for returning to Rome.

On the opposite side of Asia Minor, that is,
on the southern shore, there was a wild and
mountainous region called Cilicia. The great
chain of mountains called Taurus approaches
here very near to the sea, and the steep confor-
mations of the land, which, in the interior, pro-

duce lofty ranges and summits, and dark valleys
and ravines, form, along the line of the shore,
capes and promontories, bounded by precipitous
sides, and with deep bays and harbors between
them. The people of Cilicia were accordingly
half sailors, half mountaineers. They built
swift galleys, and made excursions in great force
over the Mediterranean Sea for conquest and
plunder. They would capture single ships, and
sometimes even whole fleets of merchantmen.
They were even strong enough on many occasions to land and take possession of a harbor and
a town, and hold it, often, for a considerable
time, against all the efforts of the neighboring
powers to dislodge them. In case, however,
their enemies became at any time too strong
for them, they would retreat to their harbors,
which were so defended by the fortresses which
guarded them, and by the desperate bravery of
the garrisons, that the pursuers generally did
not dare to attempt to force their way in; and
if, in any case, a town or a port was taken, the
indomitable savages would continue their retreat to the fastnesses of the mountains, where
it was utterly useless to attempt to follow them.

But with all their prowess and skill as naval
combatants, and their hardihood as mountain-

eers, the Cilicians lacked one thing which is
very essential in every nation to an honorable
military fame. They had no poets or historians of their own, so that the story of their deeds
had to be told to posterity by their enemies.
If they had been able to narrate their own exploits, they would have figured, perhaps, upon
the page of history as a small but brave and efficient maritime power, pursuing for many
years a glorious career of conquest, and acquiring imperishable renown by their enterprise
and success. As it was, the Romans, their enemies, described their deeds and gave them
their designation. They called them robbers
and pirates; and robbers and pirates they must
forever remain.

And it is, in fact, very likely true that the
Cilician commanders did not pursue their conquests and commit their depredations on the
rights and the property of others in quite so
systematic and methodical a manner as some
other conquering states have done. They probably seized private property a little more un-
ceremoniously than is customary; though all
belligerent nations, even in these Christian ages
of the world, feel at liberty to seize and confis-
cate private property when they find it afloat

at sea, while, by a strange inconsistency, they respect it on the land. The Cilician pirates considered themselves at war with all mankind, and, whatever merchandise they found passing from port to port along the shores of the Mediterranean, they considered lawful spoil. They intercepted the corn which was going from Sicily to Rome, and filled their own granaries with it. They got rich merchandise from the ships of Alexandria, which brought, sometimes, gold, and gems, and costly fabrics from the East; and they obtained, often, large sums of money by seizing men of distinction and wealth, who were continually passing to and fro between Italy and Greece, and holding them for a ransom. They were particularly pleased to get possession in this way of Roman generals and officers of state, who were going out to take the command of armies, or who were returning from their provinces with the wealth which they had accumulated there.

Many expeditions were fitted out and many naval commanders were commissioned to suppress and subdue these common enemies of mankind, as the Romans called them. At one time, while a distinguished general, named Antonius, was in pursuit of them at the head

of a fleet, a party of the pirates made a descent
upon the Italian coast, south of Rome, at Ni-
cenum, where the ancient patrimonial mansion
of this very Antonius was situated, and took
away several members of his family as captives,
and so compelled him to ransom them by paying a very large sum of money. The pirates
grew bolder and bolder in proportion to their
success. They finally almost stopped all intercourse between Italy and Greece, neither the
merchants daring to expose their merchandise,
nor the passengers their persons to such dangers
They then approached nearer and nearer to
Rome, and at last actually entered the Tiber,
and surprised and carried off a Roman fleet
which was anchored there. Cæsar himself fell
into the hands of these pirates at some time
during the period of his wanderings.

The pirates captured the ship in which he
was sailing near Pharmacusa, a small island
in the northeastern part of the Ægean Sea. He
was not at this time in the destitute condition
in which he had found himself on leaving Rome,
but was traveling with attendants suitable to
his rank, and in such a style and manner as at
once made it evident to the pirates that he was
a man of distinction. They accordingly held

him for ransom, and, in the mean time, until he could take measures for raising the money, they kept him a prisoner on board the vessel which had captured him.

In this situation, Cæsar, though entirely in the power and at the mercy of his lawless captors, assumed such an air of superiority and command in all his intercourse with them as at first awakened their astonishment, then excited their admiration, and ended in almost subjecting them to his will. He asked them what they demanded for his ransom. They said twenty talents, which was quite a large amount, a talent itself being a considerable sum of money. Cæsar laughed at this demand, and told them it was plain that they did not know who he was. He would give them *fifty* talents. He then sent away his attendants to the shore, with orders to proceed to certain cities where he was known, in order to procure the money, retaining only a physician and two servants for himself. While his messengers were gone, he remained on board the ship of his captors, assuming in every respect the air and manner of their master. When he wished to sleep, if they made a noise which disturbed him, he sent them orders to be still. He joined them in their sports and diversions

31—4

on the deck, surpassing them in their feats, and
taking the direction of every thing as if he were
tneir acknowledged leader.   He wrote orations
and verses which he read to them, and if his
wild auditors did not appear to appreciate the
literary excellence of his compositions, he told
them that they were stupid fools without any
taste, adding, by way of apology, that nothing
better could be expected of such barbarians.

The pirates asked him one day what he should
do to them if he should ever, at any future time,
take them prisoners.   Cæsar said that he would
crucify every one of them.

The ransom money at length arrived.   Cæsar
paid it to the pirates, and they, faithful to their
covenant, sent him in a boat to the land.   He
was put ashore on the coast of Asia Minor.   He
proceeded immediately to Miletus, the near-
est port, equipped a small fleet there, and put
to sea.   He sailed at once to the roadstead
where the pirates had been lying, and found
them still at anchor there, in perfect security.*
He attacked them, seized their ships, recovered
his ransom money, and took the men all prisoners.   He conveyed his captives to the land,
and there fulfilled his threat that he would cru-

* See Frontispiece.

cify them by cutting their throats and nailing their dead bodies to crosses which his men erected for the purpose along the shore.

During his absence from Rome Cæsar went to Rhodes, where his former preceptor resided, and he continued to pursue there for some time his former studies. He looked forward still to appearing one day in the Roman Forum. In fact, he began to receive messages from his friends at home that they thought it would be safe for him to return. Sylla had gradually withdrawn from power, and finally had died. The aristocratical party were indeed still in the ascendency, but the party of Marius had begun to recover a little from the total overthrow with which Sylla's return, and his terrible military vengeance, had overwhelmed them. Cæsar himself, therefore, they thought, might, with prudent management, be safe in returning to Rome.

He returned, but not to be prudent or cautious; there was no element of prudence or caution in his character. As soon as he arrived, he openly espoused the popular party. His first public act was to arraign the governor of the great province of Macedonia, through which he had passed on his way to Bithynia. It was

a consul whom he thus impeached, and a strong
partisan of Sylla's. His name was Dolabella.
The people were astonished at his daring in thus
raising the standard of resistance to Sylla's power, indirectly, it is true, but none the less really on that account. When the trial came on,
and Cæsar appeared at the Forum, he gained
great applause by the vigor and force of his or.
atory. There was, of course, a very strong and
general interest felt in the case; the people all
seeming to understand that, in this attack on
Dolabella, Cæsar was appearing as their champion, and their hopes were revived at having at
last found a leader capable of succeeding Marius, and building up their cause again. Dolabella was ably defended by orators on the other side, and was, of course, acquitted, for the
power of Sylla's party was still supreme. All
Rome, however, was aroused and excited by the
boldness of Cæsar's attack, and by the extraordinary ability which he evinced in his mode of
conducting it. He became, in fact, at once
one of the most conspicuous and prominent
men in the city.

Encouraged by his success, and the applaus-
es which he received, and feeling every day a
greater and greater consciousness of power, he

began to assume more and more openly the
character of the leader of the popular party.
He devoted himself to public speaking in the
Forum, both before popular assemblies and in
the courts of justice, where he was employed a
great deal as an advocate to defend those who
were accused of political crimes.   The people,
considering him as their rising champion, were
predisposed to regard every thing that he did
with favor, and there was really a great intellectual power displayed in his orations and harangues.   He acquired, in a word, great celebrity by his boldness and energy, and his boldness and energy were themselves increased in
their turn as he felt the strength of his position
increase with his growing celebrity.

At length the wife of Marius, who was Cæsar's aunt, died.   She had lived in obscurity
since her husband's proscription and death, his
party having been put down so effectually that
it was dangerous to appear to be her friend
Cæsar, however, made preparations for a magnificent funeral for her.   There was a place in
the Forum, a sort of pulpit, where public orators
were accustomed to stand in addressing the assembly on great occasions.   This pulpit was
adorned with the brazen beaks of ships which

had been taken by the Romans in former wars
The name of such a beak was *rostrum ;* in the
plural, *rostra.* The pulpit was itself, therefore,
called the *Rostra,* that is, The Beaks; and the
people were addressed from it on great public
occasions.* Cæsar pronounced a splendid panegyric upon the wife of Marius, at this her funeral, from the Rostra, in the presence of a vast
concourse of spectators, and he had the boldness to bring out and display to the people certain household images of Marius, which had
been concealed from view ever since his death.
Producing them again on such an occasion was
annulling, so far as a public orator could do it,
the sentence of condemnation which Sylla and
the patrician party had pronounced against him,
and bringing him forward again as entitled to
public admiration and applause. The patrician
partisans who were present attempted to re-
buke this bold maneuver with expressions of dis-
approbation, but these expressions were drowned in the loud and long-continued bursts of ap
plause with which the great mass of the assembled multitude hailed and sanctioned it. The
experiment was very bold and very hazardous,
but it was triumphantly successful.

* In modern books this pulpit is sometimes called the Rostrum, using the word in the singular.

A short time after this Cæsar had another
opportunity for delivering a funeral oration ; it
was in the case of his own wife, the daughter
of Cinna, who had been the colleague and co-
adjutor of Marius during the days of his power.
It was not usual to pronounce such panegyrics
upon Roman ladies unless they had attained
to an advanced age.   Cæsar, however, was disposed to make the case of his own wife an exception to the ordinary rule.   He saw in the
occasion an opportunity to give a new impulse
to the popular cause, and to make further progress in gaining the popular favor.   The experiment was successful in this instance too.   The
people were pleased at the apparent affection
which his action evinced ; and as Cornelia was
the daughter of Cinna, he had opportunity, under pretext of praising the birth and parentage
of the deceased, to laud the men whom Sylla's
party had outlawed and destroyed.   In a word,
the patrician party saw with anxiety and dread
that Cæsar was rapidly consolidating and organ-
izing, and bringing back to its pristine strength
and vigor, a party whose restoration to power
would of course involve their own political, and
perhaps personal ruin.

Cæsar began soon to receive appointments to

public office, and thus rapidly increased his influence and power.   Public officers and candi-
dates for office were accustomed in those days
to expend great sums of money in shows and
spectacles to amuse the people.   Cæsar went
beyond all limits in these expenditures.   He
brought gladiators from distant provinces, and
trained them at great expense, to fight in the
enormous amphitheaters of the city, in the
midst of vast assemblies of men.   Wild beasts
were procured also from the forests of Africa,
and brought over in great numbers, under his
direction, that the people might be entertained
by their combats with captives taken in war,
who were reserved for this dreadful fate.   Cæsar gave, also, splendid entertainments, of the
most luxurious and costly character, and he
mingled with his guests at these entertainments,
and with the people at large on other occasions,
in so complaisant and courteous a manner as to
gain universal favor.

He soon, by these means, not only exhausted
a.l his own pecuniary resources, but plunged
himself enormously into debt.   It was not difficult for such a man in those days to procure
an almost unlimited credit for such purposes as
these, for every one knew that, if he finally suc-

ceeded in placing himself, by means of the popularity thus acquired, in stations of power, he could soon indemnify himself and all others who had aided him. The peaceful merchants, and artisans, and husbandmen of the distant provinces over which he expected to rule, would yield the revenues necessary to fill the treasuries thus exhausted. Still, Cæsar's expenditures were so lavish, and the debts he incurred were so enormous, that those who had not the most unbounded confidence in his capacity and his powers believed him irretrievably ruined.

The particulars, however, of these difficulties, and the manner in which Cæsar contrived to extricate himself from them, will be more fully detailed in the next chapter.

58   JULIUS CÆSAR.   [B.C. 67

Cæsar's rise to power.   Government of Rome

CHAPTER III.

ADVANCEMENT TO THE CONSULSHIP.

FROM this time, which was about sixty·
seven years before the birth of Christ, Cæsar
remained for nine years generally at Rome, en·
gaged there in a constant struggle for power.
He was successful in these efforts, rising all the
time from one position of influence and honor to
another, until he became altogether the most
prominent and powerful man in the city. A
great many incidents are recorded, as attending
these contests, which illustrate in a very striking
manner the strange mixture of rude violence and
legal formality by which Rome was in those
days governed.

Many of the most important offices of the
state depended upon the votes of the people;
and as the people had very little opportunity to
become acquainted with the real merits of the
case in respect to questions of government, they
gave their votes very much according to the
personal popularity of the candidate. Public
men had very little moral principle in those

days, and they would accordingly resort to any means whatever to procure this personal popularity.   They who wanted office were accustomed to bribe influential men among the people to support them, sometimes by promising them subordinate offices, and sometimes by the direct donation of sums of money ; and they would try to please the mass of the people, who were too numerous to be paid with offices or with gold, by shows and spectacles, and entertainments of every kind which they would provide for their amusement.

This practice seems to us very absurd ; and we wonder that the Roman people should tolerate it, since it is evident that the means for defraying these expenses must come, ultimately, in some way or other, from them.   And yet, absurd as it seems, this sort of policy is not wholly disused even in our day.   The operas and the theaters, and other similar establishments in France, are sustained, in part, by the government ; and the liberality and efficiency with which this is done, forms, in some degree, the basis of the popularity of each succeeding administration.   The plan is better systematized and regulated in our day, but it is, in its nature, substantially the same.

In fact, furnishing amusements for the people, and also providing supplies for their wants, as well as affording them protection, were considered the legitimate objects of government in those days. It is very different at the present time, and especially in this country. The whole community are now united in the desire to confine the functions of government within the narrowest possible limits, such as to include only the preservation of public order and public safety. The people prefer to supply their own wants and to provide their own enjoyments, rather than to invest government with the power to do it for them, knowing very well that, on the latter plan, the burdens they will have to bear, though concealed for a time, must be doubled in the end.

It must not be forgotten, however, that there were some reasons in the days of the Romans for providing public amusements for the people on an extended scale which do not exist now. They had very few facilities then for the private and separate enjoyments of home, so that they were much more inclined than the people of this country are now to seek pleasure abroad and in public. The climate, too, mild and genial nearly all the year, favored this. Then they were not interested, as men are now, in the pursuits and avocations of private industry. The people of Rome were not a community of merchants, manufacturers, and citizens, enriching themselves, and adding to the comforts and enjoyments of the rest of mankind by the products of their labor. They were supported, in a great measure, by the proceeds of the tribute of foreign provinces, and by the plunder taken by the generals in the name of the state in foreign wars. From the same source, too—foreign conquest—captives were brought home, to be trained as gladiators to amuse them with their combats, and statues and paintings to ornament the public buildings of the city. In the same manner, large quantities of corn, which had been taken in the provinces, were often distributed at Rome. And sometimes even land itself, in large tracts, which had been confiscated by the state, or otherwise taken from the original possessors, was divided among the people. The laws enacted from time to time for this purpose were called Agrarian laws; and the phrase afterward passed into a sort of proverb, inasmuch as plans proposed in modern times for conciliating the favor of the populace by sharing among them property belonging to the state or to the rich, are designated by the name of *Agrarianism.*

Thus Rome was a city supported, in a great measure, by the fruits of its conquests, that is, in a certain sense, by plunder. It was a vast community most efficiently and admirably organized for this purpose ; and yet it would not be perfectly just to designate the people simply as a band of robbers. They rendered, in some sense, an equivalent for what they took, in establishing and enforcing a certain organization of society throughout the world, and in preserving a sort of public order and peace. They built cities, they constructed aqueducts and roads ; they formed harbors, and protected them by piers and by castles; they protected commerce, and cultivated the arts, and encouraged literature, and enforced a general quiet and peace among mankind, allowing of no violence or war except what they themselves created. Thus they *governed* the world, and they felt, as all governors of mankind always do, fully entitled to supply themselves with the comforts and conveniences of life, in consideration of the service which they thus rendered.

Of course, it was to be expected that they would sometimes quarrel among themselves about the spoils. Ambitious men were always arising, eager to obtain opportunities to make

fresh conquests, and to bring home new supplies, and those who were most successful in
making the results of their conquests available
in adding to the wealth and to the public enjoyments of the city, would, of course, be most
popular with the voters.   Hence extortion in
the provinces, and the most profuse and lavish
expenditure in the city, became the policy which
every great man must pursue to rise to power.

Cæsar entered into this policy with his whole
soul, founding all his hopes of success upon the
favor of the populace.   Of course, he had many
rivals and opponents among the patrician ranks,
and in the Senate, and they often impeded and
thwarted his plans and measures for a time,
though he always triumphed in the end.

One of the first offices of importance to which
he attained was that of *quæstor*, as it was called, which office called him away from Rome
into the province of Spain, making him the second in command there.   The officer first in
command in the province was, in this instance,
a prætor.   During his absence in Spain, Cæsar replenished in some degree his exhausted
finances, but he soon became very much dis-
contented with so subordinate a position.   His
discontent was greatly increased by his com-

ing unexpectedly, one day, at a city then called
Hades—the present Cadiz—upon a statue of
Alexander, which adorned one of the public edifices there.   Alexander died when he was only
about thirty years of age, having before that
period made himself master of the world.   Cæsar was himself now about thirty-five years of
age, and it made him very sad to reflect that,
though he had lived five years longer than Alexander, he had yet accomplished so little.   He
was thus far only the second in a province,
while he burned with an insatiable ambition to
be the first in Rome.   The reflection made hir
so uneasy that he left his post before his time
expired, and went back to Rome, forming, on
the way, desperate projects for getting power
there.

His rivals and enemies accused him of various schemes, more or less violent and treasona-
ble in their nature, but how justly it is not now
possible to ascertain.   They alleged that one of
his plans was to join some of the neighboring col-
onies, whose inhabitants wished to be admitted
to the freedom of the city, and, making common cause with them, to raise an armed force
and take possession of Rome.   It was said that,
to prevent the accomplishment of this design,

B.C. 65–60.] MADE CONSUL. 65

Cæsar accused of treason.   He is made ædile

an army which they had raised for the purpose
of an expedition against the Cilician pirates
was detained from its march, and that Cæsar,
seeing that the government were on their guard
against him, abandoned the plan.

They also charged him with having formed,
after this, a plan within the city for assassina-
ting the senators in the senate house, and then
usurping, with his fellow-conspirators, the supreme power. Crassus, who was a man of vast
wealth and a great friend of Cæsar's, was associated with him in this plot, and was to have
been made dictator if it had succeeded. But,
notwithstanding the brilliant prize with which
Cæsar attempted to allure Crassus to the enterprise, his courage failed him when the time
for action arrived. Courage and enterprise, in
fact, ought not to be expected of the rich ; they
are the virtues of poverty.

Though the Senate were thus jealous and
suspicious of Cæsar, and were charging him
continually with these criminal designs, the
people were on his side ; and the more he was
hated by the great, the more strongly he became
intrenched in the popular favor. They chose
him *ædile*. The ædile had the charge of the
public edifices of the city, and of the games

31—5

spectacles, and shows which were exhibited in
them.   Cæsar entered with great zeal into the
discharge of the duties of this office.   He made
arrangements for the entertainment of the people on the most magnificent scale, and made
great additions and improvements to the public buildings, constructing porticoes and piazzas
around the areas where his gladiatorial shows
and the combats with wild beasts were to be
exhibited.   He provided gladiators in such numbers, and organized and arranged them in such
a manner, ostensibly for their training, that his
enemies among the nobility pretended to believe
that he was intending to use them as an armed
force against the government of the city.   They
accordingly made laws limiting and restricting
the number of the gladiators to be employed.
Cæsar then exhibited his shows on the reduced
scale which the new laws required, taking care
that the people should understand to whom the
responsibility for this reduction in the sca'e of
their pleasures belonged.   They, of course, murmured against the Senate, and Cæsar stood
higher in their favor than ever.

He was getting, however, by these means,
very deeply involved in debt; and, in order
partly to retrieve his fortunes in this respect,

he made an attempt to have Egypt assigned to him as a province.   Egypt was then an immensely rich and fertile country.   It had, however, never been a Roman province.   It was an independent kingdom, in alliance with the Romans, and Cæsar's proposal that it should be assigned to him as a province appeared very extraordinary.   His pretext was, that the people of Egypt had recently deposed and expelled their king, and that, consequently, the Romans might properly take possession of it.   The Senate, however, resisted this plan, either from jealousy of Cæsar or from a sense of justice to Egypt; and, after a violent contest, Cæsar found himself compelled to give up the design. He felt, however, a strong degree of resentment against the patrician party who had thus thwarted his designs.   Accordingly, in order to avenge himself upon them, he one night replaced certain statues and trophies of Marius in the Capitol, which had been taken down by order of Sylla when he returned to power.   Marius, as will be recollected, had been the great champion of the popular party, and the enemy of the patricians; and, at the time of his downfall, all the memorials of his power and greatness had been every where removed from Rome.

and among them these statues and trophies,
which had been erected in the Capitol in com-
memoration of some former victories, and had
remained there until Sylla's triumph, when
they were taken down and destroyed. Cæsar
now ordered new ones to be made, far more
magnificent than before. They were made
secretly, and put up in the night. His office
as ædile gave him the necessary authority.
The next morning, when the people saw these
splendid monuments of their great favorite restored, the whole city was animated with excitement and joy. The patricians, on the other
hand, were filled with vexation and rage. "Here
is a single officer," said they, "who is attempting to restore, by his individual authority, what
has been formally abolished by a decree of the
Senate. He is trying to see how much we will
bear. If he finds that we will submit to this,
he will attempt bolder measures still." They
accordingly commenced a movement to have
the statues and trophies taken down again, but
the people rallied in vast numbers in defense of
them. They made the Capitol ring with their
shouts of applause; and the Senate, finding their
power insufficient to cope with so great a force,
gave up the point, and Cæsar gained the day.

Cæsar had married another wife after the
death of Cornelia.   Her name was Pompeia.
He divorced Pompeia about this time, under
very extraordinary circumstances.   Among the
other strange religious ceremonies and celebrations which were observed in those days, was
one called the celebration of the mysteries of the
Good Goddess.   This celebration was held by
females alone, every thing masculine being most
carefully excluded.   Even the pictures of men,
if there were any upon the walls of the house
where the assembly was held, were covered.
The persons engaged spent the night together
in music and dancing and various secret ceremonies, half pleasure, half worship, according
to the ideas and customs of the time.

The mysteries of the Good Goddess were to
be celebrated one night at Cæsar's house, he
himself having, of course, withdrawn.   In the
middle of the night, the whole company in one
of the apartments were thrown into consternation at finding that one of their number was a
man.   He had a smooth and youthful-looking
face, and was very perfectly disguised in the
dress of a female.   He proved to be a certain
Clodius, a very base and dissolute young man,
though of great wealth and high connections

He had been admitted by a female slave of Pompeia's, whom he had succeeded in bribing. It was suspected that it was with Pompeia's concurrence. At any rate, Cæsar immediately divorced his wife. The Senate ordered an inquiry into the affair, and, after the other members of the household had given their testimony, Cæsar himself was called upon, but he had nothing to say. He knew nothing about it. They asked him, then, why he had divorced Pompeia, unless he had some evidence for believing her guilty He replied, that a wife of Cæsar must not only be without crime, but without suspicion.

Clodius was a very desperate and lawless character, and his subsequent history shows, in a striking point of view, the degree of violence and disorder which reigned in those times. He became involved in a bitter contention with another citizen whose name was Milo, and each, gaining as many adherents as he could, at length drew almost the whole city into their quarrel. Whenever they went out, they were attended with armed bands, which were continually in danger of coming into collision. The collision at last came, quite a battle was fought, and Clodius was killed. This made the difficulty worse than it was before. Parties were formed, and violent disputes arose on the question of bringing Milo to trial for the alleged murder. He was brought to trial at last, but so great was the public excitement, that the consuls for the time surrounded and filled the whole Forum with armed men while the trial was proceeding, to ensure the safety of the court.

In fact, violence mingled itself continually, in those times, with almost all public proceedings, whenever any special combination of circumstances occurred to awaken unusual excitement. At one time, when Cæsar was in office, a very dangerous conspiracy was brought to light, which was headed by the notorious Catiline. It was directed chiefly against the Senate and the higher departments of the government; it contemplated, in fact, their utter destruction, and the establishment of an entirely new government on the ruins of the existing constitution. Cæsar was himself accused of a participation in this plot. When it was discovered, Catiline himself fled; some of the other conspirators were, however, arrested, and there was a long and very excited debate in the Senate on the question of their punishment. Some were for death. Cæsar, however, very earnestly opposed this plan, recommending, in-

stead, the confiscation of the estates of the conspirators, and their imprisonment in some of the
distant cities of Italy.   The dispute grew very
warm, Cæsar urging his point with great perseverance and determination, and with a degree
of violence which threatened seriously to ob-
struct the proceedings, when a body of armed
men, a sort of guard of honor stationed there,
gathered around him, and threatened him with
their swords.   Quite a scene of disorder and
terror ensued.   Some of the senators arose
hastily and fled from the vicinity of Cæsar's
seat to avoid the danger.   Others, more coura-
geous, or more devoted in their attachment to
him, gathered around him to protect him, as far
as they could, by interposing their bodies between his person and the weapons of his assailants.   Cæsar soon left the Senate, and for a
long time would return to it no more.

Although Cæsar was all this time, on the
whole, rising in influence and power, there were
still fluctuations in his fortune, and the tide
sometimes, for a short period, went strongly
against him.   He was at one time, when greatly
involved in debt, and embarrassed in all his affairs, a candidate for a very high office, that of
Pontifex Maximus, or sovereign pontiff.   The

B.C. 65–60.] MADE CONSUL. 73

Cæsar's struggle for the office of pontifex maximus.   He is deposed.

office of the pontifex was originally that of building and keeping custody of the bridges of the city, the name being derived from the Latin word *pons*, which signifies bridge.   To this, however, had afterward been added the care of the temples, and finally the regulation and control of the ceremonies of religion, so that it came in the end to be an office of the highest dignity and honor.   Cæsar made the most desperate efforts to secure his election, resorting to such measures, expending such sums, and involving himself in debt to such an extreme, that, if he failed, he would be irretrievably ruined. His mother, sympathizing with him in his anxiety, kissed him when he went away from the house on the morning of the election, and bade him farewell with tears.   He told her that he should come home that night the pontiff, or he should never come home at all.   He succeeded in gaining the election.

At one time Cæsar was actually deposed from a high office which he held, by a decree of the Senate.   He determined to disregard this decree, and go on in the discharge of his office as usual.   But the Senate, whose ascendency was now, for some reason, once more established, prepared to prevent him by force of arms

Cæsar, finding that he was not sustained, gave
up the contest, put off his robes of office, and
went home.   Two days afterward a reaction
occurred.   A mass of the populace came together to his house, and offered their assistance
to restore his rights and vindicate his honor.
Cæsar, however, contrary to what every one
would have expected of him, exerted his influence to calm and quiet the mob, and then
sent them away, remaining himself in private
as before.   The Senate had been alarmed at
the first outbreak of the tumult, and a meeting
had been suddenly convened to consider what
measures to adopt in such a crisis.   When, however, they found that Cæsar had himself interposed, and by his own personal influence had
saved the city from the danger which threatened it, they were so strongly impressed with a
sense of his forbearance and generosity, that
they sent for him to come to the senate house,
and, after formally expressing their thanks, they
canceled their former vote, and restored him to
his office again.   This change in the action of
the Senate does not, however, necessarily indicate so great a change of individual sentiment
as one might at first imagine.   There was, undoubtedly, a large minority who were averse

to his being deposed in the first instance but,
being outvoted, the decree of deposition was
passed. Others were, perhaps, more or less
doubtful. Cæsar's generous forbearance in refusing the offered aid of the populace carried
over a number of these sufficient to shift the
majority, and thus the action of the body was
reversed. It is in this way that the sudden and
apparently total changes in the action of delib-
erative assemblies which often take place, and
which would otherwise, in some cases, be almost incredible, are to be explained.

After this, Cæsar became involved in another
difficulty, in consequence of the appearance of
some definite and positive evidence that he was
connected with Catiline in his famous conspiracy. One of the senators said that Catiline
himself had informed him that Cæsar was one
of the accomplices of the plot. Another witness, named Vettius, laid an information against
Cæsar before a Roman magistrate, and offered
to produce Cæsar's handwriting in proof of
his participation in the conspirator's designs
Cæsar was very much incensed, and his manner
of vindicating himself from these serious charges
was as singular as many of his other deeds. He
arrested Vettius, and sentenced nim to pay a

heavy fine, and to be imprisoned ; and he contrived also to expose him, in the course of the
proceedings, to the mob in the Forum, who
were always ready to espouse Cæsar's cause,
and who, on this occasion, beat Vettius so un-
mercifully, that he barely escaped with his life.
The magistrate, too, was thrown into prison for
having dared to take an information against a
superior officer.

At last Cæsar became so much involved in
debt, through the boundless extravagance of his
expenditures, that something must be done to
replenish his exhausted finances.   He had, however, by this time, risen so high in official influence and power, that he succeeded in having
Spain assigned to him as his province, and he
began to make preparations to proceed to it.
His creditors, however, interposed, unwilling to
let him go without giving them security.   In
this dilemma, Cæsar succeeded in making an
arrangement with Crassus, who has already
been spoken of as a man of unbounded wealth
and great ambition, but not possessed of any
considerable degree of intellectual power.   Crassus consented to give the necessary security,
with an understanding that Cæsar was to re-
pay him by exerting his political influence in

his favor. So soon as this arrangement was made, Cæsar set off in a sudden and private manner, as if he expected that otherwise some new difficulty would intervene.

He went to Spain by land, passing through Switzerland on the way. He stopped with his attendants one night at a very insignificant village of shepherds' huts among the mountains. Struck with the poverty and worthlessness of all they saw in this wretched hamlet, Cæsar's friends were wondering whether the jealousy, rivalry, and ambition which reigned among men every where else in the world could find any footing there, when Cæsar told them that, for his part, he should rather choose to be first in such a village as that than the second at Rome. The story has been repeated a thousand times, and told to every successive generation now for nearly twenty centuries, as an illustration of the peculiar type and character of the ambition which controls such a soul as that of Cæsar.

Cæsar was very successful in the administration of his province; that is to say, he returned in a short time with considerable military glory, and with money enough to pay all his debts, and furnish him with means for fresh electioneering.

He now felt strong enough to aspire to the
office of consul, which was the highest office of
the Roman state.   When the line of kings had
been deposed, the Romans had vested the supreme magistracy in the hands of two consuls,
who were chosen annually in a general election,
the formalities of which were all very carefully
arranged.   The current of popular opinion was,
of course, in Cæsar's favor, but he had many
powerful rivals and enemies among the great,
who, however, hated and opposed each other as
well as him.   There was at that time a very
bitter feud between Pompey and Crassus, each
of them struggling for power against the efforts
of the other.   Pompey possessed great influence
through his splendid abilities and his military
renown.   Crassus, as has already been stated,
was powerful through his wealth.   Cæsar, who
had some influence with them both, now conceived the bold design of reconciling them, and
then of availing himself of their united aid in
accomplishing his own particular ends.

He succeeded perfectly well in this management.   He represented to them that, by contending against each other, they only exhausted
their own powers, and strengthened the arms
of their common enemies.   He proposed to them

to unite with one another and with him, and
thus make common cause to promote their common interest and advancement.   They willingly
acceded to this plan, and a triple league was accordingly formed, in which they each bound
themselves to promote, by every means in his
power, the political elevation of the others, and
not to take any public step or adopt any measures without the concurrence of the three.
Cæsar faithfully observed the obligations of this
league so long as he could use his two associates to promote his own ends, and then he abandoned it.

Having, however, completed this arrangement, he was now prepared to push vigorously
his claims to be elected consul.   He associated
with his own name that of Lucceius, who was
a man of great wealth, and who agreed to defray
the expenses of the election for the sake of the
honor of being consul with Cæsar.   Cæsar's enemies, however, knowing that they probably
would not prevent his election, determined to
concentrate their strength in the effort to prevent his having the colleague he desired.   They
made choice, therefore, of a certain Bibulus as
their candidate.   Bibulus had always been a
political opponent of Cæsar's, and they thought

that, by associating him with Cæsar in the supreme magistracy, the pride and ambition of their great adversary might be held somewhat in check. They accordingly made a contribution among themselves to enable Bibulus to expend as much money in bribery as Lucceius, and the canvass went on.

It resulted in the election of Cæsar and Bibulus. They entered upon the duties of their office; but Cæsar, almost entirely disregarding his colleague, began to assume the whole power, and proposed and carried measure after measure of the most extraordinary character, all aiming at the gratification of the populace. He was at first opposed violently both by Bibulus and by many leading members of the Senate, especially by Cato, a stern and inflexible patriot, whom neither fear of danger nor hope of reward could move from what he regarded his duty. But Cæsar was now getting strong enough to put down the opposition which he encountered without much scruple as to the means. He ordered Cato on one occasion to be arrested in the Senate and sent to prison. Another influential member of the Senate rose and was going out with him. Cæsar asked him where he was going. He said he was going with Cato. He would rather, he said, be with Cato in prison, than in the Senate with Cæsar.

Cæsar treated Bibulus also with so much neglect, and assumed so entirely the whole control of the consular power, to the utter exclusion of his colleague, that Bibulus at last, completely discouraged and chagrined, abandoned all pretension to official authority, retired to his house, and shut himself up in perfect seclusion, leaving Cæsar to his own way.   It was customary among the Romans, in their historical and narrative writings, to designate the successive years, not by a numerical date as with us, but by the names of the consuls who held office in them.   Thus, in the time of Cæsar's consulship, the phrase would have been, "In the year of Cæsar and Bibulus, consuls," according to the ordinary usage; but the wags of the city, in order to make sport of the assumptions of Cæsar and the insignificance of Bibulus, used to say, "In the year of Julius and Cæsar, consuls," rejecting the name of Bibulus altogether, and taking the two names of Cæsar to make out the necessary duality

31—6

CHAPTER IV.

THE CONQUEST OF GAUL.

IN attaining to the consulship, Cæsar had reached the highest point of elevation which it was possible to reach as a mere citizen of Rome. His ambition was, however, of course, not satisfied. The only way to acquire higher distinction and to rise to higher power was to enter upon a career of foreign conquest. Cæsar therefore aspired now to be a soldier. He accordingly obtained the command of an army, and entered upon a course of military campaigns in the heart of Europe, which he continued for eight years. These eight years constitute one of the most important and strongly-marked periods of his life. He was triumphantly successful in his military career, and he made, accordingly, a vast accession to his celebrity and power, in his own day, by the results of his campaigns. He also wrote, himself, an account of his adventures during this period, in which the events are recorded in so lucid and in so eloquent a manner, that the narrations have con-

tinued to be read by every successive generation of scholars down to the present day, and
they have had a great influence in extending
and perpetuating his fame.

The principal scenes of the exploits which
Cæsar performed during the period of this his
first great military career, were the north of
Italy, Switzerland, France, Germany, and England, a great tract of country, nearly all of
which he overran and conquered. A large portion of this territory was called Gaul in those
days; the part on the Italian side of the Alps
being named Cisalpine Gaul, while that which
lay beyond was designated as Transalpine.
Transalpine Gaul was substantially what is
now France. There was a part of Transalpine
Gaul which had been already conquered and
reduced to a Roman province. It was called
The Province then, and has retained the name,
with a slight change in orthography, to the present day. It is now known as Provence.

The countries which Cæsar went to invade
were occupied by various nations and tribes,
many of which were well organized and war-
like, and some of them were considerably civilized and wealthy. They had extended tracts
of cultivated land, the slopes of the hills and the

84　　　　Julius Cæsar　　[B.C. 58–50

Condition of Gaul in Cæsar's day.　　　　　Singular cavalry

mountain sides being formed into green pastu-
rages, which were covered with flocks of goats,
and sheep, and herds of cattle, while the smooth-
er and more level tracts were adorned with
smiling vineyards and broadly-extended fields
of waving grain.　They had cities, forts, ships,
and armies.　Their manners and customs would
be considered somewhat rude by modern nations, and some of their usages of war were half
barbarian.　For example, in one of the nations
which Cæsar encountered, he found, as he says
in his narrative, a corps of cavalry, as a constituent part of the army, in which, to every
horse, there were *two* men, one the rider, and
the other a sort of foot soldier and attendant
If the battle went against them, and the squadron were put to their speed in a retreat, these
footmen would cling to the manes of the horses,
and then, half running, half flying, they would
be borne along over the field, thus keeping always at the side of their comrades, and escaping
with them to a place of safety.

But, although the Romans were inclined to
consider these nations as only half civilized, still
there would be great glory, as Cæsar thought,
in subduing them, and probably great treasure
would be secured in the conquest, both by the

)lunder and confiscation of governmental property, and by the tribute which would be collected in taxes from the people of the countries
subdued. Cæsar accordingly placed himself at
the head of an army of three Roman legions,
which he contrived, by means of a great deal
of political maneuvering and management, to
have raised and placed under his command.
One of these legions, which was called the tenth
legion, was his favorite corps, on account of the
bravery and hardihood which they often displayed. At the head of these legions, Cæsar
set out for Gaul. He was at this time not far
from forty years of age.

Cæsar had no difficulty in finding pretexts for
making war upon any of these various nations
that he might desire to subdue. They were,
of course, frequently at war with each other,
and there were at all times standing topics of
controversy and unsettled disputes among them.
Cæsar had, therefore, only to draw near to the
scene of contention, and then to take sides with
one party or the other, it mattered little with
which, for the affair almost always resulted, in
the end, in his making himself master of both.
The manner, however, in which this sort of operation was performed, can best be illustrated

by an example, and we will take for the purpose the case of Ariovistus.

Ariovistus was a German king. He had
been nominally a sort of ally of the Romans.
He had extended his conquests across the Rhine
into Gaul, and he held some nations there as
his tributaries.   Among these, the Æduans
were a prominent party, and, to simplify the
account, we will take their name as the representative of all who were concerned.   When
Cæsar came into the region of the Æduans, he
entered into some negotiations with them, in
which they, as he alleges, asked his assistance
to enable them to throw off the dominion of
their German enemy.   It is probable, in fact,
that there was some proposition of this kind
from them, for Cæsar had abundant means of
inducing them to make it, if he was disposed ;
and the receiving of such a communication
furnished the most obvious and plausible pretext to authorize and justify his interposition.

Cæsar accordingly sent a messenger across
the Rhine to Ariovistus, saying that he wished
to have an interview with him on business of
importance, and asking him to name a time
which would be convenient to him for the interview, and also to appoint some place in Gaul
where he would attend

To this Ariovistus replied, that if he had, himself, any business with Cæsar, he would have waited upon him to propose it; and, in the same manner, if Cæsar wished to see him, he must come into his own dominions. He said that it would not be safe for him to come into Gaul without an army, and that it was not convenient for him to raise and equip an army for such a purpose at that time.

Cæsar sent again to Ariovistus to say, that since he was so unmindful of his obligations to the Roman people as to refuse an interview with him on business of common interest, he would state the particulars that he required of him. The Æduans, he said, were now his allies, and under his protection; and Ariovistus must send back the hostages which he held from them, and bind himself henceforth not to send any more troops across the Rhine, nor make war upon the Æduans, or injure them in any way. If he complied with these terms, all would be well. If he did not, Cæsar said that he should not himself disregard the just complaints of his allies.

Ariovistus had no fear of Cæsar. Cæsar had, in fact, thus far, not begun to acquire the military renown to which he afterward attained

Ariovistus had, therefore, no particular cause
to dread his power.   He sent him back word
that he did not understand why Cæsar should
interfere between him and his conquered province.   " The Æduans," said he, " tried the fortune of war with me, and were overcome ; and
they must abide the issue. The Romans manage their conquered provinces as they judge
proper, without holding themselves accountable
to any one.   I shall do the same with mine.
All that I can say is, that so long as the Æduans submit peaceably to my authority, and pay
their tribute, I shall not molest them ; as to
your threat that you shall not disregard their
complaints, you must know that no one has
ever made war upon me but to his own destruction, and, if you wish to see how it will turn out
in your case, you may make the experiment
whenever you please."

Both parties immediately prepared for war.
Ariovistus, instead of waiting to be attacked,
assembled his army, crossed the Rhine, and advanced into the territories from which Cæsar
had undertaken to exclude him.

As Cæsar, however, began to make his arrangements for putting his army in motion to
meet his approaching enemy, there began to cir-

culate throughout the camp such extraordinary
stories of the terrible strength and courage of
the German soldiery as to produce a very general panic. So great, at length, became the
anxiety and alarm, that even the officers were
wholly dejected and discouraged; and as for the
men, they were on the very eve of mutiny.

When Cæsar understood this state of things,
he called an assembly of the troops, and made
an address to them. He told them that he was
astonished to learn to what an extent an un-
worthy despondency and fear had taken possession of their minds, and how little confidence
they reposed in him, their general. And then,
after some further remarks about the duty of a
soldier to be ready to go wherever his commander leads him, and presenting also some considerations in respect to the German troops with
which they were going to contend, in order to
show them that they had no cause to fear, he
ended by saying that he had not been fully decided as to the time of marching, but that now
he had concluded to give orders for setting out
the next morning at three o'clock, that he might
learn, as soon as possible, who were too coward-
ly to follow him. He would go himself, he said,
if he was attended by the tenth legion alone

He was sure that they would not shrink from any undertaking in which he led the way.

The soldiers, moved partly by shame, partly by the decisive and commanding tone which their general assumed, and partly reassured by the courage and confidence which he seemed to feel, laid aside their fears, and vied with each other henceforth in energy and ardor. The armies approached each other. Ariovistus sent to Cæsar, saying that now, if he wished it, he was ready for an interview. Cæsar acceded to the suggestion, and the arrangements for a conference were made, each party, as usual in such cases, taking every precaution to guard against the treachery of the other.

Between the two camps there was a rising ground, in the middle of an open plain, where it was decided that the conference should be held. Ariovistus proposed that neither party should bring any foot soldiers to the place of meeting, but cavalry alone; and that these bodies of cavalry, brought by the respective generals, should remain at the foot of the eminence on either side, while Cæsar and Ariovistus themselves, attended each by only ten followers on horseback, should ascend it. This plan was acceded to by Cæsar, and a long conference was held in

B.C. 58–50.] CONQUEST OF GAUL. 91

Conference between Cæsar and Ariovistus. Cæsar's messenger seized.

this way between the two generals, as they sat upon their horses, on the summit of the hill.

The two generals, in their discussion, only repeated in substance what they had said in their embassages before, and made no progress toward coming to an understanding. At length Cæsar closed the conference and withdrew. Some days afterward Ariovistus sent a request to Cæsar, asking that he would appoint another interview, or else that he would depute one of his officers to proceed to Ariovistus's camp and receive a communication which he wished to make to him. Cæsar concluded not to grant another interview, and he did not think it prudent to send any one of his principal officers as an embassador, for fear that he might be treacherously seized and held as a hostage. He accordingly sent an ordinary messenger, accompanied by one or two men. These men were all seized and put in irons as soon as they reached the camp of Ariovistus, and Cæsar now prepared in earnest for giving his enemy battle.

He proved himself as skillful and efficient in arranging and managing the combat as he had been sagacious and adroit in the negotiations which preceded it. Several days were spent in maneuvers and movements, by which each

party endeavored to gain some advantage over
the other in respect to their position in the approaching struggle.   When at length the combat came, Cæsar and his legions were entirely
and triumphantly successful.   The Germans
were put totally to flight.   Their baggage and
stores were all seized, and the troops themselves
fled in dismay by all the roads which led back
to the Rhine; and there those who succeeded
in escaping death from the Romans, who pursued them all the way, embarked in boats and
upon rafts, and returned to their homes.   Ariovistus himself found a small boat, in which,
with one or two followers, he succeeded in getting across the stream.

As Cæsar, at the head of a body of his troops,
was pursuing the enemy in this their flight, he
overtook one party who had a prisoner with
them confined by iron chains fastened to his
limbs, and whom they were hurrying rapidly
along.   This prisoner proved to be the messenger that Cæsar had sent to Ariovistus's camp,
and whom he had, as Cæsar alleges, treacherously detained.   Of course, he was overjoyed to
be recaptured and set at liberty.   The man
said that three times they had drawn lots to see
whether they should burn him alive then, or re-

serve the pleasure for a future occasion, and
that every time the lot had resulted in his favor.

The consequence of this victory was, that
Cæsar's authority was established triumphantly
over all that part of Gaul which he had thus
freed from Ariovistus's sway. Other parts of
the country, too, were pervaded by the fame of
his exploits, and the people every where began
to consider what action it would be incumbent
on them to take, in respect to the new military
power which had appeared so suddenly among
them. Some nations determined to submit
without resistance, and to seek the conqueror's
alliance and protection. Others, more bold,
or more confident of their strength, began to
form combinations and to arrange plans for resisting him. But, whatever they did, the result in the end was the same. Cæsar's ascendency was every where and always gaining
ground. Of course, it is impossible in the compass of a single chapter, which is all that can
be devoted to the subject in this volume, to
give any regular narrative of the events of the
eight years of Cæsar's military career in Gaul.
Marches, negotiations, battles, and victories
mingled with and followed each other in a long
succession, the particulars of which it would re-

quire a volume to detail, every thing resulting most successfully for the increase of Cæsar's power and the extension of his fame.

Cæsar gives, in his narrative, very extraordinary accounts of the customs and modes of life of some of the people that he encountered. There was one country, for example, in which all the lands were common, and the whole structure of society was based on the plan of forming the community into one great martial band. The nation was divided into a hundred cantons, each containing two thousand men capable of bearing arms. If these were all mustered into service together, they would form, of course, an army of two hundred thousand men. It was customary, however, to organize only one half of them into an army, while the rest remained at home to till the ground and tend the flocks and herds. These two great divisions interchanged their work every year, the soldiers becoming husbandmen, and the husbandmen soldiers. Thus they all became equally inured to the hardships and dangers of the camp, and to the more continuous but safer labors of agricultural toil. Their fields were devoted to pasturage more than to tillage, for flocks and herds could be driven from place to place, and thus

B.C. 58–50.] Conquest of Gaul. 95

Well-trained horses.   Cæsar's popularity with the army

more easily preserved from the depredations of
enemies than fields of grain. The children grew
up almost perfectly wild from infancy, and hard-
ened themselves by bathing in cold streams,
wearing very little clothing, and making long
hunting excursions among the mountains. The
people had abundance of excellent horses, which
the young men were accustomed, from their
earliest years, to ride without saddle or bridle,
the horses being trained to obey implicitly every
command. So admirably disciplined were they,
that sometimes, in battle, the mounted men
would leap from their horses and advance as
foot soldiers to aid the other infantry, leaving
the horses to stand until they returned. The
horses would not move from the spot; the men,
when the object for which they had dismounted
was accomplished, would come back, spring to
their seats again, and once more become a squadron of cavalry.

Although Cæsar was very energetic and decided in the government of his army, he was
extremely popular with his soldiers in all these
campaigns. He exposed his men, of course, to
a great many privations and hardships, but then
he evinced, in many cases, such a willingness
to bear his share of them, that the men were

very little inclined to complain.   He moved at
the head of the column when his troops were
advancing on a march, generally on horseback,
but often on foot; and Suetonius says that he
used to go bareheaded on such occasions. whatever was the state of the weather, though it is
difficult to see what the motive of this appa
rently needless exposure could be, unless it was
for effect, on some special or unusual occasion.
Cæsar would ford or swim rivers with his men
whenever there was no other mode of transit,
sometimes supported, it was said, by bags in-
flated with air, and placed under his arms.   At
one time he built a bridge across the Rhine, to
enable his army to cross that river.   This bridge
was built with piles driven down into the sand,
which supported a flooring of timbers.   Cæsar,
considering it quite an exploit thus to bridge
the Rhine, wrote a minute account of the manner in which the work was constructed, and the
description is almost exactly in accordance with
the principles and usages of modern carpentry.

After the countries which were the scene of
these conquests were pretty well subdued, Cæsar established on some of the great routes of
travel a system of posts, that is, he stationed
supplies of horses at intervals of from ten to

twenty miles along the way, so that he himself, or the officers of his army, or any couriers whom he might have occasion to send with dispatches could travel with great speed by finding a fresh horse ready at every stage. By this means he sometimes traveled himself a hund~ed miles in a day. This system, thus adopted for military purposes in Cæsar's time, has been continued in almost all countries of Europe to the present age, and is applied to traveling in carriages as well as on horseback. A family party purchase a carriage, and arranging within it all the comforts and conveniences which they will require on the journey, they set out, taking these post horses, fresh at each village, to draw them to the next. Thus they can go at any rate of speed which they desire, instead of being limited in their movements by the powers of endurance of one set of animals, as they would be compelled to be if they were to travel with their own. This plan has, for some reason, never been introduced into America, and it is now probable that it never will be, as the railway system will doubtless supersede it.

One of the most remarkable of the enterprises which Cæsar undertook during the period of these campaigns was his excursion into Great

Britain.   The real motive of this expedition
was probably a love of romantic adventure,
and a desire to secure for himself at Rome the
glory of having penetrated into remote regions
which Roman armies had never reached before.
The pretext, however, which he made to justify
his invading the territories of the Britons was,
that the people of the island were accustomed
to come across the Channel and aid the Gauls
in their wars.

In forming his arrangements for going into
England, the first thing was, to obtain all the
information which was accessible in Gaul in respect to the country.   There were, in those days,
great numbers of traveling merchants, who went
from one nation to another to purchase and sell,
taking with them such goods as were most easy
of transportation.   These merchants, of course,
were generally possessed of a great deal of information in respect to the countries which they
had visited, and Cæsar called together as many
of them as he could find, when he had reached
the northern shores of France, to inquire about
the modes of crossing the Channel, the harbors
on the English side, the geographical conforma-
tion of the country, and the military resources
of the people.   He found, however, that the

merchants could give him very little information. They knew that Britain was an island, but they did not know its extent or its boundaries; and they could tell him very little of the character or customs of the people. They said that they had only been accustomed to land upon the southern shore, and to transact all their business there, without penetrating at all into the interior of the country.

Cæsar then, who, though undaunted and bold in emergencies requiring prompt and decisive action, was extremely cautious and wary at all other times, fitted up a single ship, and, putting one of his officers on board with a proper crew, directed him to cross the Channel to the English coast, and then to cruise along the land for some miles in each direction, to observe where were the best harbors and places for landing, and to examine generally the appearance of the shore. This vessel was a galley, manned with numerous oarsmen, well selected and strong, so that it could retreat with great speed from any sudden appearance of danger The name of the officer who had the command of it was Volusenus. Volusenus set sail, the army watching his vessel with great interest as 't moved slowly away from the shore. He was gone five days, and then returned, bringing Cæsar an account of his discoveries.

In the mean time, Cæsar had collected a large number of sailing vessels from the whole line of the French shore, by means of which he proposed to transport his army across the Channel. He had two legions to take into Britain, the remainder of his forces having been stationed as garrisons in various parts of Gaul. It was necessary, too, to leave a considerable force at his post of debarkation, in order to secure a safe retreat in case of any disaster on the British side. The number of transport ships provided for the foot soldiers which were to be taken over was eighty. There were, besides these, eighteen more, which were appointed to convey a squadron of horse. This cavalry force was to embark at a separate port, about eighty miles distant from the one from which the infantry were to sail.

At length a suitable day for the embarkation arrived; the troops were put on board the ships, and orders were given to sail. The day could not be fixed beforehand, as the time for attempting to make the passage must necessarily depend upon the state of the wind and weather. Accordingly, when the favorable opportunity arrived, and the main body of the army began to embark it took some time to send the orders to the port where the cavalry had rendezvoused; and there were, besides, other causes of delay which occurred to detain this corps, so that it turned out, as we shall presently see, that the foot soldiers had to act alone in the first attempt at landing on the British shore.

It was one o'clock in the morning when the fleet set sail. The Britons had, in the mean time, obtained intelligence of Cæsar's threatened invasion, and they had assembled in great force, with troops, and horsemen, and carriages of war, and were all ready to guard the shore. The coast, at the point where Cæsar was approaching, consists of a line of chalky cliffs, with valley-like openings here and there between them, communicating with the shore, and sometimes narrow beaches below. When the Roman fleet approached the land, Cæsar found the cliffs every where lined with troops of Britons, and every accessible point below carefully guarded. It was now about ten o'clock in the morning, and Cæsar, finding the prospect so unfavorable in respect to the practicability of effecting a landing here, brought

his fleet to anchor near the shore, but far
enough from it to be safe from the missiles of
the enemy.

Here he remained for several hours, to give
time for all the vessels to join him. Some of
them had been delayed in the embarkation, or
had made slower progress than the rest in crossing the Channel. He called a council, too, of
the superior officers of the army on board his
own galley, and explained to them the plan
which he now adopted for the landing. About
three o'clock in the afternoon he sent these officers back to their respective ships, and gave
orders to make sail along the shore. The anchors were raised and the fleet moved on, borne
by the united impulse of the wind and the tide.
The Britons, perceiving this movement, put
themselves in motion on the land, following the
motions of the fleet so as to be ready to meet
their enemy wherever they might ultimately
undertake to land. Their horsemen and carriages went on in advance, and the foot soldiers
followed, all pressing eagerly forward to keep
up with the motion of the fleet, and to prevent
Cæsar's army from having time to land before
they should arrive at the spot and be ready to
oppose them.

The Landing in England.

The fleet moved on until, at length, after sailing about eight miles, they came to a part of the coast where there was a tract of comparatively level ground, which seemed to be easily accessible from the shore. Here Cæsar determined to attempt to land; and drawing up his vessel, accordingly, as near as possible to the beach, he ordered the men to leap over into the water, with their weapons in their hands. The Britons were all here to oppose them, and a dreadful struggle ensued, the combatants dyeing the waters with their blood as they fought, half submerged in the surf which rolled in upon the sand. Some galleys rowed up at the same time near to the shore, and the men on board of them attacked the Britons from the decks, by the darts and arrows which they shot to the land. Cæsar at last prevailed; the Britons were driven away, and the Roman army established themselves in quiet possession of the shore.

Cæsar had afterward a great variety of adventures, and many narrow escapes from imminent dangers in Britain, and, though he gained considerable glory by thus penetrating into such remote and unknown regions, there was very little else to be acquired. The glory, however, was itself of great value to Cæsar. During the whole period of his campaigns in Gaul, Rome, and all Italy in fact, had been filled with the fame of his exploits, and the expedition into Britain added not a little to his renown. The populace of the city were greatly gratified to hear of the continued success of their former favorite. They decreed to him triumph after triumph, and were prepared to welcome him, whenever he should return, with greater honors and more extended and higher powers than he had ever enjoyed before.

Cæsar's exploits in these campaigns were, in fact, in a military point of view, of the most magnificent character. Plutarch, in summing up the results of them, says that he took eight hundred cities, conquered three hundred nations, fought pitched battles at separate times with three millions of men, took one million of prisoners, and killed another million on the field. What a vast work of destruction was this for a man to spend eight years of his life in performing upon his fellow-creatures, merely to gratify his insane love of dominion.

Chapter V.

Pompey.

WHILE Cæsar had thus been rising to so high an elevation, there was another Roman general who had been, for nearly the same period, engaged, in various other quarters of the world, in acquiring, by very similar means, an almost equal renown. This general was Pompey. He became, in the end, Cæsar's great and formidable rival. In order that the reader may understand clearly the nature of the great contest which sprung up at last between these heroes, we must now go back and relate some of the particulars of Pompey's individual history down to the time of the completion of Cæsar's conquests in Gaul.

Pompey was a few years older than Cæsar, having been born in 106 B.C. His father was a Roman general, and the young Pompey was brought up in camp. He was a young man of very handsome figure and countenance, and of very agreeable manners. His hair curled slightly over his forehead, and he had a dark

and intelligent eye, full of vivacity and meaning.   There was, besides, in the expression of
his face, and in his air and address, a certain
indescribable charm, which prepossessed every
one strongly in his favor, and gave him, from
his earliest years, a great personal ascendency
over all who knew him.

Notwithstanding this popularity, however,
Pompey did not escape, even in very early life,
incurring his share of the dangers which seemed
to environ the path of every public man in those
distracted times.   It will be recollected that, in
the contests between Marius and Sylla, Cæsar
had joined the Marian faction.   Pompey's father, on the other hand, had connected himself
with that of Sylla.   At one time, in the midst
of these wars, when Pompey was very young,
a conspiracy was formed to assassinate his father by burning him in his tent, and Pompey's
comrade, named Terentius, who slept in the
same tent with him, had been bribed to kill
Pompey himself at the same time, by stabbing
him in his bed.   Pompey contrived to discover
this plan, but, instead of being at all discom-
posed by it, he made arrangements for a guard
about his father's tent, and then went to supper
as usual with Terentius, conversing with him

all the time in even a more free and friendly
manner than usual.   That night he arranged
his bed so as to make it appear as if he was in
it, and then stole away.   When the appointed
hour arrived, Terentius came into the tent, and,
approaching the couch where he supposed Pompey was lying asleep, stabbed it again and again,
piercing the coverlets in many places, but doing
no harm, of course, to his intended victim.

In the course of the wars between Marius
and Sylla, Pompey passed through a great variety of scenes, and met with many extraordinary adventures and narrow escapes, which,
however, can not be here particularly detailed.
His father, who was as much hated by his soldiers as the son was beloved, was at last, one
day, struck by lightning in his tent.   The soldiers were inspired with such a hatred for his
memory, in consequence, probably, of the cruelties and oppressions which they had suffered
from him, that they would not allow his body
to be honored with the ordinary funeral obse-
quies.   They pulled it off from the bier on
which it was to have been borne to the funeral
pile, and dragged it ignominiously away.   Pompey's father was accused, too, after his death,
of having converted some public moneys which

had been committed to his charge to his own
use, and Pompey appeared in the Roman Forum as an advocate to defend him from the
charge and to vindicate his memory. He was
very successful in this defense. All who heard
it were, in the first instance, very deeply interested in favor of the speaker, on account of his
extreme youth and his personal beauty; and,
as he proceeded with his plea, he argued with
so much eloquence and power as to win universal applause. One of the chief officers of the
government in the city was so much pleased
with his appearance, and with the promise of
future greatness which the circumstances indicated, that he offered him his daughter in mar
riage. Pompey accepted the offer, and married
the lady. Her name was Antistia.

Pompey rose rapidly to higher and higher de-
grees of distinction, until he obtained the command of an army, which he had, in fact, in a
great measure raised and organized himself, and
he fought at the head of it with great energy
and success against the enemies of Sylla. At
length he was hemmed in on the eastern coast
of Italy by three separate armies, which were
gradually advancing against him, with a cer-
tainty, as they thought, of effecting his destruc-

tion. Sylla, hearing of Pompey's danger, made great efforts to march to his rescue. Before he reached the place, however, Pompey had met and defeated one after another of the armies of his enemies, so that, when Sylla approached, Pompey marched out to meet him with his army drawn up in magnificent array, trumpets sounding and banners flying, and with large bodies of disarmed troops, the prisoners that he had taken, in the rear. Sylla was struck with surprise and admiration; and when Pompey saluted him with the title of *Imperator*, which was the highest title known to the Roman constitution, and the one which Sylla's lofty rank and unbounded power might properly claim, Sylla returned the compliment by conferring this great mark of distinction on him.

Pompey proceeded to Rome, and the fame of his exploits, the singular fascination of his person and manners, and the great favor with Sylla that he enjoyed, raised him to a high degree of distinction. He was not, however, elated with the pride and vanity which so young a man would be naturally expected to exhibit under such circumstances. He was, on the contrary, modest and unassuming, and he acted in all respects in such a manner as to gain the appro-

bation and the kind regard of all who knew him,
as well as to excite their applause.   There was
an old general at this time in Gaul—for all these
events took place long before the time of Cæsar's
campaigns in that country, and, in fact, before
the commencement of his successful career in
Rome—whose name was Metellus, and who,
either on account of his advancing age, or for
some other reason, was very inefficient and unsuccessful in his government.   Sylla proposed
to supersede him by sending Pompey to take
his place.   Pompey replied that it was not right
to take the command from a man who was so
much his superior in age and character, but
that, if Metellus wished for his *assistance* in the
management of his command, he would proceed
to Gaul and render him every service in his
power.   When this answer was reported to Metellus, he wrote to Pompey to come.   Pompey
accordingly went to Gaul, where he obtained
new victories, and gained new and higher honors
than before.

These, and various anecdotes which the ancient historians relate, would lead us to form
very favorable ideas of Pompey's character.
Some other circumstances, however, which occurred, seem to furnish different indications

For example, on his return to Rome, some time
after the events above related, Sylla, whose estimation of Pompey's character and of the importance of his services seemed continually to
increase, wished to connect him with his own
family by marriage. He accordingly proposed
that Pompey should divorce his wife Antistia,
and marry Æmilia, the daughter-in-law of Sylla. Æmilia was already the wife of another
man, from whom she would have to be taken
away to make her the wife of Pompey. This,
however, does not seem to have been thought
a very serious difficulty in the way of the arrangement. Pompey's wife was put away, and
the wife of another man taken in her place.
Such a deed was a gross violation not merely
of revealed and written law, but of those universal instincts of right and wrong which are
implanted indelibly in all human hearts. It
ended, as might have been expected, most dis-
astrously. Antistia was plunged, of course,
into the deepest distress. Her father had recently lost his life on account of his supposed
attachment to Pompey. Her mother killed
herself in the anguish and despair produced by
the misfortunes of her family; and Æmilia
the new wife, died suddenly, on the occasion

of the birth of a child, a very short time after her marriage with Pompey.

These domestic troubles did not, however, interpose any serious obstacle to Pompey's progress in his career of greatness and glory. Sylla sent him on one great enterprise after another, in all of which Pompey acquitted himself in an admirable manner. Among his other campaigns, he served for some time in Africa with great success. He returned in due time from this expedition, loaded with military honors. His soldiers had become so much attached to him that there was almost a mutiny in the army when he was ordered home. They were determined to submit to no authority but that of Pompey. Pompey at length succeeded, by great efforts, in subduing this spirit, and bringing back the army to their duty. A false account of the affair, however, went to Rome. It was reported to Sylla that there was a revolt in the army of Africa, headed by Pompey himself, who was determined not to resign his command. Sylla was at first very indignant that his authority should be despised and his power braved, as he expressed it, by "such a boy;" for Pompey was still, at this time, very young. When, however, he learned the truth, he con-

ceived a higher admiration for the young general than ever. He went out to meet him as
he approached the city, and, in accosting him,
he called him Pompey the Great. Pompey has
continued to bear the title thus given him to
the present day.

Pompey began, it seems, now to experience,
in some degree, the usual effects produced upon
the human heart by celebrity and praise. He
demanded a triumph. A triumph was a great
and splendid ceremony, by which victorious gen
erals, who were of advanced age and high civil
or military rank, were received into the city
when returning from any specially glorious campaign. There was a grand procession formed
on these occasions, in which various emblems
and insignia, and trophies of victory, and cap
tives taken by the conqueror, were displayed.
This great procession entered the city with
bands of music accompanying it, and flags and
banners flying, passing under triumphal arches
erected along the way. Triumphs were usually decreed by a vote of the Senate, in cases
where they were deserved; but, in this case,
Sylla's power as dictator was supreme, and
Pompey's demand for a triumph seems to have
been addressed accordingly to him.

Sylla refused it. Pompey's performances in the African campaign had been, he admitted. very creditable to him, but he had neither the age nor the rank to justify the granting him a triumph. To bestow such an honor upon one so young and in such a station, would only bring the honor itself, he said, into disrepute, and degrade, also, his dictatorship for suffering it.

To this Pompey replied, speaking, however, in an under tone to those around him in the assembly, that Sylla need not fear that the triumph would be unpopular, for people were much more disposed to worship a rising than a setting sun. Sylla did not hear this remark, but, perceiving by the countenances of the by-standers that Pompey had said something which seemed to please them, he asked what it was. When the remark was repeated to him, he seemed pleased himself with its justness or with its wit, and said, "Let him have his triumph."

The arrangements were accordingly made. Pompey ordering every thing necessary to be prepared for a most magnificent procession. He learned that some persons in the city, envious at his early renown, were displeased with his triumph; this only awakened in him a determ

ination to make it still more splendid and imposing. He had brought some elephants with
him from Africa, and he formed a plan for having the car in which he was to ride in the procession drawn by four of these huge beasts as
it entered the city; but, on measuring the gate,
it was found not wide enough to admit such a
team, and the plan was accordingly abandoned
The conqueror's car was drawn by horses in
the usual manner, and the elephants followed
singly, with the other trophies, to grace the
train.

Pompey remained some time after this in
Rome, sustaining from time to time various offices of dignity and honor. His services were
often called for to plead causes in the Forum,
and he performed this duty, whenever he undertook it, with great success. He, however,
seemed generally inclined to retire somewhat
from intimate intercourse with the mass of the
community, knowing very well that if he was
engaged often in the discussion of common
questions with ordinary men, he should soon
descend in public estimation from the high position to which his military renown had raised
him. He accordingly accustomed himself to
appear but little in public, and, when he did so

appear, he was generally accompanied by a large retinue of armed attendants, at the head of which he moved about the city in great state, more like a victorious general in a conquered province than like a peaceful citizen exercising ordinary official functions in a community governed by law. This was a very sagacious course, so far as concerned the attainment of the great objects of future ambition. Pompey knew very well that occasions would probably arise in which he could act far more effectually for the promotion of his own greatness and fame than by mingling in the ordinary municipal contests of the city.

At length, in fact, an occasion came. In the year B.C. 67, which was about the time that Cæsar commenced his successful career in rising to public office in Rome, as is described in the third chapter of this volume, the Cilician pirates, of whose desperate character and bold exploits something has already been said, had become so powerful, and were increasing so rapidly in the extent of their depredations, that the Roman people felt compelled to adopt some very vigorous measures for suppressing them. The pirates had increased in numbers during the wars between Marius and Sylla in a very

alarming degree.   They had built, equipped,
and organized whole fleets.   They had various
fortresses, arsenals, ports, and watch-towers all
along the coasts of the Mediterranean.   They
had also extensive warehouses, built in secure
and secluded places, where they stored their
plunder.   Their fleets were well manned, and
provided with skillful pilots, and with ample
supplies of every kind; and they were so well
constructed, both for speed and safety, that no
other ships could be made to surpass them.
Many of them, too, were adorned and decora-
ted in the most sumptuous manner, with gilded sterns, purple awnings, and silver-mounted
oars.   The number of their galleys was said to
be a thousand.   With this force they made
themselves almost complete masters of the sea.
They attacked not only separate ships, but
whole fleets of merchantmen sailing under con-
voy; and they increased the difficulty and expense of bringing grain to Rome so much, by
intercepting the supplies, as very materially to
enhance the price and to threaten a scarcity.
They made themselves masters of many isl-
ands and of various maritime towns along the
coast, until they had four hundred ports and
ties in their possession.   In fact, they had

gone so far toward forming themselves into a regular maritime power, under a systematic and legitimate government, that very respectable young men from other countries began to enter their service, as one opening honorable avenues to wealth and fame.

Under these circumstances, it was obvious that something decisive must be done. A friend of Pompey's brought forward a plan for commissioning some one, he did not say whom, but every one understood that Pompey was intended, to be sent forth against the pirates, with extraordinary powers, such as should be amply sufficient to enable him to bring their dominion to an end. He was to have supreme command upon the sea, and also upon the land for fifty miles from the shore. He was, moreover, to be empowered to raise as large a force, both of ships and men, as he should think required, and to draw from the treasury whatever funds were necessary to defray the enormous expenses which so vast an undertaking would involve. If the law should pass creating this office and a person be designated to fill it, it is plain that such a commander would be clothed with enormous powers; but then he would incur, on the other hand, a vast and commensu-

rate responsibility, as the Roman people would
hold him rigidly accountable for the full and
perfect accomplishment of the work he under
took, after they had thus surrendered every pos
sible power necessary to accomplish it so un
conditionally into his hands.

There was a great deal of maneuvering, management, and debate on the one hand to effect
the passage of this law, and, on the other, to defeat it. Cæsar, who, though not so prominent
yet as Pompey, was now rising rapidly to influence and power, was in favor of the measure, because, as is said, he perceived that the
people were pleased with it. It was at length
adopted. Pompey was then designated to fill
the office which the law created. He accepted
the trust, and began to prepare for the vast undertaking. The price of grain fell immediately
in Rome, as soon as the appointment of Pompey was made known, as the merchants, who
had large supplies in the granaries there, were
now eager to sell, even at a reduction, feeling
confident that Pompey's measures would result
in bringing in abundant supplies. The people,
surprised at this sudden relaxation of the press-
ure of their burdens, said that the very name
of Pompey had put an end to the war.

They were not mistaken in their anticipations of Pompey's success. He freed the Mediterranean from pirates in three months, by one systematic and simple operation, which affords one of the most striking examples of the power of united and organized effort, planned and conducted by one single master mind, which the history of ancient or modern times has recorded. The manner in which this work was effected was this:

Pompey raised and equipped a vast number of galleys, and divided them into separate fleets, putting each one under the command of a lieutenant. He then divided the Mediterranean Sea into thirteen districts, and appointed a lieutenant and his fleet for each one of them as a guard. After sending these detachments forth to their respective stations, he set out from the city himself to take charge of the operations which he was to conduct in person. The people followed him, as he went to the place where he was to embark, in great crowds, and with long and loud acclamations.

Beginning at the Straits of Gibraltar, Pompey cruised with a powerful fleet toward the east, driving the pirates before him, the lieutenants, who were stationed along the coast,

being on the alert to prevent them from finding
any places of retreat or refuge. Some of the
pirates' ships were surrounded and taken. Others fled, and were followed by Pompey's ships
until they had passed beyond the coasts of Sicily, and the seas between the Italian and African shores. The communication was now open
again to the grain-growing countries south of
Rome, and large supplies of food were immediately poured into the city. The whole population was, of course, filled with exultation and
joy at receiving such welcome proofs that Pompey was successfully accomplishing the work
they had assigned him.

The Italian peninsula and the island of Sicily,
which are, in fact, a projection from the northern shores of the Mediterranean, with a salient
angle of the coast nearly opposite to them on
the African side, form a sort of strait which di
vides this great sea into two separate bodies of
water, and the pirates were now driven entirely out of the western division. Pompey sent
his principal fleet after them, with orders to
pass around the island of Sicily and the south
ern part of Italy to Brundusium, which was the
great port on the western side of Italy. He
nimself was to cross the peninsula by land, tak

ing Rome in his way, and afterward to join the
fleet at Brundusium.　The pirates, in the mean
time, so far as they had escaped Pompey's
cruisers, had retreated to the seas in the neighborhood of Cilicia, and were concentrating their
forces there in preparation for the final struggle.

Pompey was received at Rome with the utmost enthusiasm.　The people came out in
throngs to meet him as he approached the city,
and welcomed him with loud acclamations.　He
did not, however, remain in the city to enjoy
these honors.　He procured, as soon as possible,
what was necessary for the further prosecution
of his work, and went on.　He found his fleet
at Brundusium, and, immediately embarking,
he put to sea.

Pompey went on to the completion of his
work with the same vigor and decision which
he had displayed in the commencement of it.
Some of the pirates, finding themselves hemmed
in within narrower and narrower limits, gave up
the contest, and came and surrendered.　Pompey, instead of punishing them severely for their
crimes, treated them, and their wives and children, who fell likewise into his power, with great
humanity.　This induced many others to follow
their example, so that the number that remained

resisting to the end was greatly reduced. There were, however, after all these submissions, a body of stern and indomitable desperadoes left, who were incapable of yielding. These retreated, with all the forces which they could retain, to their strong-holds on the Silician shores, sending their wives and children back to still securer retreats among the fastnesses of the mountains.

Pompey followed them, hemming them in with the squadrons of armed galleys which he brought up around them, thus cutting off from them all possibility of escape. Here, at length, a great final battle was fought, and the dominion of the pirates was ended forever. Pompey destroyed their ships, dismantled their fortifications, restored the harbors and towns which they had seized to their rightful owners, and sent the pirates themselves, with their wives and children, far into the interior of the country, and established them as agriculturists and herdsmen there, in a territory which he set apart for the purpose, where they might live in peace on the fruits of their own industry, without the possibility of again disturbing the commerce of the seas.

Instead of returning to Rome after these ex

126   JULIUS CÆSAR.   [B.C. 50

Pompey's conquests in Asia Minor.   His magnificent triumph.

ploits, Pompey obtained new powers from the
government of the city, and pushed his way into
Asia Minor, where he remained several years,
pursuing a similar career of conquest to that
of Cæsar in Gaul. At length he returned to
Rome, his entrance into the city being signalized by a most magnificent triumph. The
procession for displaying the trophies, the captives, and the other emblems of victory, and for
conveying the vast accumulation of treasures
and spoils, was two days in passing into the
city; and enough was left after all for another
triumph. Pompey was, in a word, on the very
summit of human grandeur and renown.

He found, however, an old enemy and rival
at Rome. This was Crassus, who had been
Pompey's opponent in earlier times, and who
now renewed his hostility. In the contest that
ensued, Pompey relied on his renown, Crassus
on his wealth. Pompey attempted to please the
people by combats of lions and of elephants
which he had brought home from his foreign
campaigns; Crassus courted their favor by dis-
tributing corn among them, and inviting them
to public feasts on great occasions. He spread
for them, at one time, it was said, ten thousand
tables. All Rome was filled with the feuds of

these great political foes.   It was at this time
that Cæsar returned from Spain, and had the
adroitness, as has already been explained, to ex-
tinguish these feuds, and reconcile these apparently implacable foes.   He united them together, and joined them with himself in a triple
league, which is celebrated in Roman history
as the first *triumvirate*.   The rivalry, however,
of these great aspirants for power was only suppressed and concealed, without being at all
weakened or changed.   The death of Crassus
soon removed him from the stage.   Cæsar and
Pompey continued afterward, for some time,
an ostensible alliance.   Cæsar attempted to
strengthen this bond by giving Pompey his
daughter Julia for his wife.   Julia, though so
young—even her father was six years younger
than Pompey—was devotedly attached to her
husband, and he was equally fond of her.   She
formed, in fact, a strong bond of union between
the two great conquerors as long as she lived.
One day, however, there was a riot at an election, and men were killed so near to Pompey
that his robe was covered with blood.   He
changed it; the servants carried home the
bloody garment which he had taken off, and
Julia was so terrified at the sight, thinking that

her husband had been killed, that she fainted,
and her constitution suffered very severely by
the shock.   She lived some time afterward, but
finally died under circumstances which indicate
that this occurrence was the cause.   Pompey
and Cæsar now soon became open enemies.
The ambitious aspirations which each of them
cherished were so vast, that the world was not
wide enough for them both to be satisfied.
They had assisted each other up the ascent
which they had been so many years in climb-
ing, but now they had reached very near to the
summit, and the question was to be decided
which of the two should have his station there.

CHAPTER VI.

CROSSING THE RUBICON.

THERE was a little stream in ancient times, in the north of Italy, which flowed westward into the Adriatic Sea, called the Rubicon. This stream has been immortalized by the transactions which we are now about to describe.

The Rubicon was a very important boundary, and yet it was in itself so small and insignificant that it is now impossible to determine which of two or three little brooks here running into the sea is entitled to its name and renown. In history the Rubicon is a grand, permanent, and conspicuous stream, gazed upon with continued interest by all mankind for nearly twenty centuries; in nature it is an uncertain rivulet, for a long time doubtful and undetermined, and finally lost.

The Rubicon originally derived its importance from the fact that it was the boundary between all that part of the north of Italy which is formed by the valley of the Po, one of the richest and most magnificent countries of the

31—9

world, and the more southern Roman territories. This country of the Po constituted what
was in those days called the *hither* Gaul, and
was a Roman province. It belonged now to
Cæsar's jurisdiction, as the commander in Gaul.
All south of the Rubicon was territory reserved
for the immediate jurisdiction of the city. The
Romans, in order to protect themselves from
any danger which might threaten their own
liberties from the immense armies which they
raised for the conquest of foreign nations, had
imposed on every side very strict limitations
and restrictions in respect to the approach of
these armies to the Capitol. The Rubicon was
the limit on this northern side. Generals commanding in Gaul were never to pass it. To
cross the Rubicon with an army on the way to
Rome was rebellion and treason. Hence the
Rubicon became, as it were, the visible sign
and symbol of civil restriction to military power.

As Cæsar found the time of his service in
Gaul drawing toward a conclusion, he turned
his thoughts more and more toward Rome, endeavoring to strengthen his interest there by
every means in his power, and to circumvent
and thwart the designs of Pompey. He had
agents and partisans in Rome who acted for

him and in his name.   He sent immense sums
of money to these men, to be employed in such
ways as would most tend to secure the favor
of the people.   He ordered the Forum to be re-
built with great magnificence.   He arranged
great celebrations, in which the people were entertained with an endless succession of games,
spectacles, and public feasts.   When his daughter Julia, Pompey's wife, died, he celebrated
her funeral with indescribable splendor.   He
distributed corn in immense quantities among
the people, and he sent a great many captives
home, to be trained as gladiators, to fight in the
theaters for their amusement.   In many cases,
too, where he found men of talents and influence among the populace, who had become involved in debt by their dissipations and extravagance, he paid their debts, and thus secured
their influence on his side.   Men were astound-
ed at the magnitude of these expenditures, and,
while the multitude rejoiced thoughtlessly in
the pleasures thus provided for them, the more
reflecting and considerate trembled at the greatness of the power which was so rapidly rising
to overshadow the land.

It increased their anxiety to observe that
Pompey was gaining the same kind of influ-

ence and ascendency too. He had not the advantage which Cæsar enjoyed in the prodigious wealth obtained from the rich countries over which Cæsar ruled, but he possessed, instead of it, the advantage of being all the time at Rome, and of securing, by his character and action there, a very wide personal popularity and influence. Pompey was, in fact, the idol of the people. At one time, when he was absent from Rome, at Naples, he was taken sick. After being for some days in considerable danger, the crisis passed favorably, and he recovered. Some of the people of Naples proposed a public thanksgiving to the gods, to celebrate his restoration to health. The plan was adopted by acclamation, and the example, thus set, extended from city to city, until it had spread throughout Italy, and the whole country was filled with the processions, games, shows, and celebrations, which were instituted every where in honor of the event. And when Pompey returned from Naples to Rome, the towns on the way could not afford room for the crowds that came forth to meet him. The high roads, the villages, the ports, says Plutarch, were filled with sacrifices and entertainments. Many received him with garlands on their heads and torches in their hands, and, as they conducted him along, strewed the way with flowers.

In fact, Pompey considered himself as standing far above Cæsar in fame and power, and this general burst of enthusiasm and applause, educed by his recovery from sickness, confirmed him in this idea. He felt no solicitude, he said, in respect to Cæsar. He should take no special precautions against any hostile designs which he might entertain on his return from Gaul. It was he himself, he said, that had raised Cæsar up to whatever of elevation he had attained, and he could put him down even more easily than he had exalted him.

In the mean time, the period was drawing near in which Cæsar's command in the provinces was to expire; and, anticipating the struggle with Pompey which was about to ensue, he conducted several of his legions through the passes of the Alps, and advanced gradually, as he had a right to do, across the country of the Po toward the Rubicon, revolving in his capacious mind, as he came, the various plans by which he might hope to gain the ascendency over the power of his mighty rival, and make aimself supreme.

He concluded that it would be his wisest

policy not to attempt to intimidate Pompey by
great and open preparations for war, which
might tend to arouse him to vigorous measures
of resistance, but rather to cover and conceal
his designs, and thus throw his enemy off his
guard.   He advanced, therefore, toward the Rubicon with a small force.   He established his
headquarters at Ravenna, a city not far from
the river, and employed himself in objects of
local interest there, in order to avert as much as
possible the minds of the people from imagining
that he was contemplating any great design.
Pompey sent to him to demand the return of
a certain legion which he had lent him from
his own army at a time when they were friends.
Cæsar complied with this demand without any
hesitation, and sent the legion home.   He sent
with this legion, also, some other troops which
were properly his own, thus evincing a degree
of indifference in respect to the amount of the
force retained under his command which seemed wholly inconsistent with the idea that he
contemplated any resistance to the authority of
the government at Rome.

In the mean time, the struggle at Rome between the partisans of Cæsar and Pompey grew
more and more violent and alarming.   Cæsar

through his friends in the city, demanded to be
elected consul. The other side insisted that he
must first, if that was his wish, resign the command of his army, come to Rome, and present
himself as a candidate in the character of a private citizen. This the constitution of the state
very properly required. In answer to this requisition, Cæsar rejoined, that, if Pompey would
lay down his military commands, he would do
so too; if not, it was unjust to require it of him
The services, he added, which he had performed
for his country, demanded some recompense,
which, moreover, they ought to be willing to
award, even if, in order to do it, it were necessary to relax somewhat in his favor the strict-
ness of ordinary rules. To a large part of the
people of the city these demands of Cæsar appeared reasonable. They were clamorous to
have them allowed. The partisans of Pompey,
with the stern and inflexible Cato at their head,
deemed them wholly inadmissible, and contend-
ed with the most determined violence against
them. The whole city was filled with the excitement of this struggle, into which all the active and turbulent spirits of the capital plunged
with the most furious zeal, while the more considerate and thoughtful of the population, re-

nembering the days of Marius and Sylla, trembled at the impending danger.   Pompey himself
had no fear.   He urged the Senate to resist to
the utmost all of Cæsar's claims, saying, if Cæsar should be so presumptuous as to attempt to
march to Rome, he could raise troops enough
by stamping with his foot to put him down.

It would require a volume to contain a full
account of the disputes and tumults, the maneuvers and debates, the votes and decrees which
marked the successive stages of this quarrel
Pompey himself was all the time without the
city.   He was in command of an army there,
and no general, while in command, was allowed to come within the gates.   At last an ex-
citing debate was broken up in the Senate by
one of the consuls rising to depart, saying that
he would hear the subject discussed no longer
The time had arrived for action, and he should
send a commander, with an armed force, to defend the country from Cæsar's threatened invasion.   Cæsar's leading friends, two tribunes
of the people, disguised themselves as slaves,
and fled to the north to join their master   The
country was filled with commotion and panic.
The Commonwealth had obviously more fear
of Cæsar than confidence in Pompey.   The

country was full of rumors in respect to Cæsar's power, and the threatening attitude which
he was assuming, while they who had insisted
on resistance seemed, after all, to have provided very inadequate means with which to resist.
A thousand plans were formed, and clamorously
insisted upon by their respective advocates, for
averting the danger. This only added to the
confusion, and the city became at length pervaded with a universal terror.

While this was the state of things at Rome,
Cæsar was quietly established at Ravenna,
thirty or forty miles from the frontier. He was
erecting a building for a fencing school there
and his mind seemed to be occupied very busily
with the plans and models of the edifice which
the architects had formed. Of course, in his
intended march to Rome, his reliance was not
to be so much on the force which he should
take with him, as on the co-operation and support which he expected to find there. It was
his policy, therefore, to move as quietly and privately as possible, and with as little display of
violence, and to avoid every thing which might
indicate his intended march to any spies which
might be around him, or to any other persons
who might be disposed to report what they ob-

served at Rome.   Accordingly, on the very eve
of his departure, he busied himself with his fencing school, and assumed with his officers and
soldiers a careless and unconcerned air, which
prevented any one from suspecting his design.

In the course of the day he privately sent
forward some cohorts to the southward, with
orders for them to encamp on the banks of the
Rubicon.   When night came he sat down to
supper as usual, and conversed with his friends
in his ordinary manner, and went with them
afterward to a public entertainment.   As soon
as it was dark and the streets were still, he
set off secretly from the city, accompanied by a
very few attendants.   Instead of making use
of his ordinary equipage, the parading of which
would have attracted attention to his movements, he had some mules taken from a neighboring bake-house, and harnessed into his chaise
There were torch-bearers provided to light the
way.   The cavalcade drove on during the night,
finding, however, the hasty preparations which
had been made inadequate for the occasion.
The torches went out, the guides lost their
way, and the future conqueror of the world
wandered about bewildered and lost, until, just
after break of day, the party met with a peas

CROSSING THE RUBICON.

ant who undertook to guide them. Under his
direction they made their way to the main
road again, and advanced then without further
difficulty to the banks of the river, where they
found that portion of the army which had been
sent forward encamped, and awaiting their arrival.

Cæsar stood for some time upon the banks
of the stream, musing upon the greatness of
the undertaking in which simply passing across
it would involve him. His officers stood by his
side. "We can retreat *now*," said he, "but
once across that river and we must go on." He
paused for some time, conscious of the vast importance of the decision, though he thought
only, doubtless, of its consequences to himself
Taking the step which was now before him
would necessarily end either in his realizing the
loftiest aspirations of his ambition, or in his ut
ter and irreparable ruin. There were vast public interests, too, at stake, of which, however
he probably thought but little. It proved, in
the end, that the history of the whole Roman
world, for several centuries, was depending upon
the manner in which the question now in Cæsar's mind should turn.

There was a little bridge across the Rubicon

at the point where Cæsar was surveying it.
While he was standing there, the story is, a
peasant or shepherd came from the neighboring
fields with a shepherd's pipe—a simple musical
instrument, made of a reed, and used much by
the rustic musicians of those days. The soldiers and some of the officers gathered around
him to hear him play. Among the rest came
some of Cæsar's trumpeters, with their trumpets
in their hands. The shepherd took one of these
martial instruments from the hands of its possessor, laying aside his own, and began to sound
a charge—which is a signal for a rapid advance
—and to march at the same time over the bridge
" An omen! a prodigy !" said Cæsar. " Let
us march where we are called by such a divine
intimation. *The die is cast.*"

So saying, he pressed forward over the bridge,
while the officers, breaking up the encampment,
put the columns in motion to follow him.

It was shown abundantly, on many occasions
in the course of Cæsar's life, that he had no
faith in omens. There are equally numerous
instances to show that he was always ready
to avail himself of the popular belief in them,
to awaken his soldiers' ardor or to allay their
fears. Whether, therefore, in respect to this

story of the shepherd trumpeter, it was an incident that really and accidentally occurred, or whether Cæsar planned and arranged it himself, with reference to its effect, or whether, which is, perhaps, after all, the most probable supposition, the tale was only an embellishment invented out of something or nothing by the story-tellers of those days, to give additional dramatic interest to the narrative of the crossing of the Rubicon, it must be left for each reader to decide.

As soon as the bridge was crossed, Cæsar called an assembly of his troops, and, with signs of great excitement and agitation, made an address to them on the magnitude of the crisis through which they were passing. He showed them how entirely he was in their power; he urged them, by the most eloquent appeals, to stand by him, faithful and true, promising them the most ample rewards when he should have attained the object at which he aimed. The soldiers responded to this appeal with promises of the most unwavering fidelity.

The first town on the Roman side of the Rubicon was Ariminum. Cæsar advanced to this town. The authorities opened its gates to him —very willing, as it appeared, to receive him as their commander. Cæsar's force was yet quite small, as he had been accompanied by only a single legion in crossing the river. He had, however, sent orders for the other legions, which had been left in Gaul, to join him without any delay, though any re-enforcement of his troops seemed hardly necessary, as he found no indications of opposition to his progress. He gave his soldiers the strictest injunctions to do no injury to any property, public or private, as they advanced, and not to assume, in any respect, a hostile attitude toward the people of the country. The inhabitants, therefore, welcomed him wherever he came, and all the cities and towns followed the example of Ariminum, surrendering, in fact, faster than he could take possession of them.

In the confusion of the debates and votes in the Senate at Rome before Cæsar crossed the Rubicon, one decree had been passed deposing him from his command of the army, and appointing a successor. The name of the general thus appointed was Domitius. The only real opposition which Cæsar encountered in his progress toward Rome was from him. Domitius had crossed the Apennines at the head of an army on his way northward to supersede Cæsar in his command, and had reached the town of Corfinium, which was perhaps one third of the way between Rome and the Rubicon. Cæsar advanced upon him here and shut him in.

After a brief siege the city was taken, and Domitius and his army were made prisoners. Every body gave them up for lost, expecting that Cæsar would wreak terrible vengeance upon them. Instead of this, he received the troops at once into his own service, and let Domitius go free.

In the mean time, the tidings of Cæsar's having passed the Rubicon, and of the triumphant success which he was meeting with at the commencement of his march toward Rome, reached the Capitol, and added greatly to the prevailing consternation. The reports of the magnitude of his force and of the rapidity of his progress were greatly exaggerated. The party of Pompey and the Senate had done every thing to spread among the people the terror of Cæsar's name, in order to arouse them to efforts for opposing his designs; and now, when he had broken through the barriers which had been intended to restrain him, and was advancing toward the city in an unchecked and triumphant career, they were overwhelmed with dismay

Pompey began to be terrified at the danger which was impending. The Senate held meetings without the city—councils of war, as it were, in which they looked to Pompey in vain for protection from the danger which he had brought upon them. He had said that he could raise an army sufficient to cope with Cæsar at any time by stamping with his foot. They told him they thought now that it was high time for him to stamp.

In fact, Pompey found the current setting every where strongly against him. Some recommended that commissioners should be sent to Cæsar to make proposals for peace. The leading men, however, knowing that any peace made with him under such circumstances would be their own ruin, resisted and defeated the proposal. Cato abruptly left the city and proceeded to Sicily, which had been assigned him as his province. Others fled in other directions. Pompey himself, uncertain what to do, and not daring to remain, called upon all his partisans to join him, and set off at night, suddenly, and with very little preparation and small supplies, to retreat across the country toward the shores of the Adriatic Sea. His destination was Brundusium, the usual port of embarkation for Macedon and Greece.

Cæsar was all this time gradually advancing toward Rome. His soldiers were full of enthusiasm in his caase.   As his connection with the government at home was sundered the moment he crossed the Rubicon, all supplies of money and of provisions were cut off in that quarter until he should arrive at the Capitol and take possession of it.   The soldiers voted, however, that they would serve him without pay. The officers, too, assembled together, and tendered him the aid of their contributions.   He had always observed a very generous policy in his dealings with them, and he was now greatly gratified at receiving their requital of it.

The further he advanced, too, the more he found the people of the country through which he passed disposed to espouse his cause.   They were struck with his generosity in releasing Domitius.   It is true that it was a very sagacious policy that prompted him to release him. But then it was generosity too.   In fact, there must be something of a generous spirit in the soul to enable a man even to see the policy of generous actions.

Among the letters of Cæsar that remain to the present day, there is one written about this time to one of his friends, in which he speaks of this subject. "I am glad," says he, "that you approve of my conduct at Corfinium. I am satisfied that such a course is the best one for us to pursue, as by so doing we shall gain the good will of all parties, and thus secure a permanent victory. Most conquerors have incurred the hatred of mankind by their cruelties, and have all, in consequence of the enmity they have thus awakened, been prevented from long enjoying their power. Sylla was an exception; but his example of successful cruelty I have no disposition to imitate. I will conquer after a new fashion, and fortify myself in the possession of the power I acquire by generosity and mercy."

Domitius had the ingratitude, after this release, to take up arms again, and wage a new war against Cæsar. When Cæsar heard of it, he said it was all right. "I will act out the principles of my nature," said he, "and he may act out his."

Another instance of Cæsar's generosity occurred, which is even more remarkable than this. It seems that among the officers of his army there were some whom he had appointed at the recommendation of Pompey, at the time when he and Pompey were friends. These men

would, of course, feel under obligations of gratitude to Pompey, as they owed their military
rank to his friendly interposition in their behalf.
As soon as the war broke out, Cæsar gave them
all his free permission to go over to Pompey's
side, if they chose to do so.

Cæsar acted thus very liberally in all respects.
He surpassed Pompey very much in the spirit
of generosity and mercy with which he entered
upon the great contest before them.   Pompey
ordered every citizen to join his standard, declaring that he should consider all neutrals as
his enemies.   Cæsar, on the other hand, gave
free permission to every one to decline, if he
chose, taking any part in the contest, saying
that he should consider all who did not act
against him as his friends.   In the political contests of our day, it is to be observed that the
combatants are much more prone to imitate the
bigotry of Pompey than the generosity of Cæsar,
condemning, as they often do, those who choose
to stand aloof from electioneering struggles, more
than they do their most determined opponents
and enemies.

When, at length, Cæsar arrived at Brundusium, he found that Pompey had sent a part of
his army across the Adriatic into Greece, and

was waiting for the transports to return that he
might go over himself with the remainder.   In
the mean time, he had fortified himself strongly
in the city   Cæsar immediately laid siege to
the place, and he commenced some works to
block up the mouth of the harbor.   He built
piers on each side, extending out as far into the
sea as the depth of the water would allow them
to be built.   He then constructed a series of
rafts, which he anchored on the deep water, in
a line extending from one pier to the other.   He
built towers upon these rafts, and garrisoned
them with soldiers, in hopes by this means to
prevent all egress from the fort.   He thought
that, when this work was completed, Pompey
would be entirely shut in, beyond all possibility
of escape.

The transports, however, returned before the
work was completed.   Its progress was, of
course, slow, as the constructions were the scene
of a continued conflict; for Pompey sent out
rafts and galleys against them every day, and the
workmen had thus to build in the midst of con-
tinual interruptions, sometimes from showers
of darts, arrows, and javelins, sometimes from
the conflagrations of fireships, and sometimes
from the terrible concussions of great vessels

of war, impelled with prodigious force against them. The transports returned, therefore, before the defenses were complete, and contrived to get into the harbor. Pompey immediately formed his plan for embarking the remainder of his army.

He filled the streets of the city with barricades and pitfalls, excepting two streets which led to the place of embarkation. The object of these obstructions was to embarrass Cæsar's progress through the city in case he should force an entrance while his men were getting on board the ships. He then, in order to divert Cæsar's attention from his design, doubled the guards stationed upon the walls on the evening of his intended embarkation, and ordered them to make vigorous attacks upon all Cæsar's forces outside. He then, when the darkness came on, marched his troops through the two streets which had been left open, to the landing place, and got them as fast as possible on board the transports. Some of the people of the town contrived to make known to Cæsar's army what was going on, by means of signals from the walls; the army immediately brought scaling ladders in great numbers, and, mounting the walls with great ardor and impetuosity, they

drove all before them, and soon broke open the
gates and got possession of the city.　But the
barricades and pitfalls, together with the darkness, so embarrassed their movements, that
Pompey succeeded in completing his embarkation and sailing away.

Cæsar had no ships in which to follow.　He
returned to Rome.　He met, of course, with no
opposition.　He re-established the government
there, organized the Senate anew, and obtained
supplies of corn from the public granaries, and of
money from the city treasury in the Capitol.　In
going to the Capitoline Hill after this treasure,
he found the officer who had charge of the money
stationed there to defend it.　He told Cæsar
that it was contrary to law for him to enter.
Cæsar said that, for men with swords in their
hands, there was no law.　The officer still re
fused to admit him.　Cæsar then told him to
open the doors, or he would kill him on the spot.
"And you must understand," he added, "that
it will be easier for me to do it than it has been
to say it."　The officer resisted no longer, and
Cæsar went in.

After this, Cæsar spent some time in vigorous campaigns in Italy, Spain, Sicily, and
Gaul, wherever there was manifested any op

position to his sway. When this work was accomplished, and all these countries were completely subjected to his dominion, he began to turn his thoughts to the plan of pursuing Pompey across the Adriatic Sea.

CHAPTER VII.

THE BATTLE OF PHARSALIA.

THE gathering of the armies of Cæsar and
Pompey on the opposite shores of the Adriatic Sea was one of the grandest preparations
for conflict that history has recorded, and the
whole world gazed upon the spectacle at the
time with an intense and eager interest, which
was heightened by the awe and terror which
the danger inspired. During the year while
Cæsar had been completing his work of subduing and arranging all the western part of the
empire, Pompey had been gathering from the
eastern division every possible contribution to
swell the military force under his command,
and had been concentrating all these elements
of power on the coasts of Macedon and Greece,
opposite to Brundusium, where he knew that
Cæsar would attempt to cross the Adriatic Sea.
His camps, his detachments, his troops of archers and slingers, and his squadrons of horse, filled the land, while every port was guarded, and
the line of the coast was environed by batteries

and castles on the rocks, and fleets of galleys on the water. Cæsar advanced with his immense army to Brundusium, on the opposite shore, in December, so that, in addition to the formidable resistance prepared for him by his enemy on the coast, he had to encounter the wild surges of the Adriatic, rolling perpetually in the dark and gloomy commotion always raised in such wide seas by wintery storms.

Cæsar had no ships, for Pompey had cleared the seas of every thing which could aid him in his intended passage. By great efforts, however, he succeeded at length in getting together a sufficient number of galleys to convey over a part of his army, provided he took the men alone, and left all his military stores and baggage behind. He gathered his army together, therefore, and made them an address, representing that they were now drawing toward the end of all their dangers and toils. They were about to meet their great enemy for a final conflict. It was not necessary to take their servants, their baggage, and their stores across the sea, for they were sure of victory, and victory would furnish them with ample supplies from those whom they were about to conquer.

The soldiers eagerly imbibed the spirit of confidence and courage which Cæsar himself expressed. A large detachment embarked and put to sea, and, after being tossed all night upon the cold and stormy waters, they approached the shore at some distance to the northward of the place where Pompey's fleets had expected them. It was at a point where the mountains came down near to the sea, rendering the coast rugged and dangerous with shelving rocks and frowning promontories. Here Cæsar succeeded in effecting a landing of the first division of his troops, and then sent back the fleet for the remainder.

The news of his passage spread rapidly to all Pompey's stations along the coast, and the ships began to gather, and the armies to march toward the point where Cæsar had effected his landing. The conflict and struggle commenced. One of Pompey's admirals intercepted the fleet of galleys on their return, and seized and burned a large number of them, with all who were on board. This, of course, only renewed the determined desperation of the remainder. Cæsar advanced along the coast with the troops which he had landed, driving Pompey's troops before him, and subduing town after town as he advanced. The country was filled with ter-

ror and dismay. The portion of the army which
Cæsar had left behind could not now cross, partly on account of the stormy condition of the
seas, the diminished number of the ships, and
the redoubled vigilance with which Pompey's
forces now guarded the shores, but mainly because Cæsar was now no longer with them to
inspire them with his reckless, though calm and
quiet daring. They remained, therefore, in
anxiety and distress, on the Italian shore. As
Cæsar, on the other hand, advanced along the
Macedonian shore, and drove Pompey back into
the interior, he cut off the communication between Pompey's ships and the land, so that the
fleet was soon reduced to great distress for want
of provisions and water. The men kept themselves from perishing with thirst by collecting
the dew which fell upon the decks of their galleys. Cæsar's army was also in distress, for
Pompey's fleets cut off all supplies by water,
and his troops hemmed them in on the side of
the land ; and, lastly, Pompey himself, with the
immense army that was under his command,
began to be struck with alarm at the impending danger with which they were threatened.
Pompey little realized, however, how dreadful
a fate was soon to overwhelm him.

The winter months rolled away, and nothing effectual was done. The forces, alternating and intermingled, as above described, kept each other in a continued state of anxiety and suffering. Cæsar became impatient at the delay of that portion of his army that he had left on the Italian shore. The messages of encouragement and of urgency which he sent across to them did not bring them over, and at length, one dark and stormy night, when he thought that the inclemency of the skies and the heavy surging of the swell in the offing would drive his vigilant enemies into places of shelter, and put them off their guard, he determined to cross the sea himself and bring his hesitating army over. He ordered a galley to be prepared, and went on board of it disguised, and with his head muffled in his mantle, intending that not even the officers or crew of the ship which was to convey him should know of his design. The galley, in obedience to orders, put off from the shore. The mariners endeavored in vain for some time to make head against the violence of the wind and the heavy concussions of the waves, and at length, terrified at the imminence of the danger to which so wild and tumultuous a sea on such a night exposed them, refused to proceed, and the commander gave them orders to return. Cæsar then came forward, threw off his mantle, and said to them, "Friends! you have nothing to fear. You are carrying Cæsar."

The men were, of course, inspirited anew by this disclosure, but all was in vain. The obstacles to the passage proved insurmountable, and the galley, to avoid certain destruction, was compelled to return.

The army, however, on the Italian side, hearing of Cæsar's attempt to return to them, fruitless though it was, and stimulated by the renewed urgency of the orders which he now sent to them, made arrangements at last for an embarkation, and, after encountering great dangers on the way, succeeded in landing in safety. Cæsar, thus strengthened, began to plan more decided operations for the coming spring.

There were some attempts at negotiation. The armies were so exasperated against each other on account of the privations and hardships which each compelled the other to suffer, that they felt too strong a mutual distrust to attempt any regular communication by commissioners or embassadors appointed for the purpose. They came to a parley, however, in one or two instances, though the interviews led to no result. As the missiles used in those days were such as could only be thrown to a very short distance, hostile bodies of men could approach much nearer to each other then than is possible now, when projectiles of the most terribly destructive character can be thrown for miles.   In one instance, some of the ships of Pompey's fleet approached so near to the shore as to open a conference with one or two of Cæsar's lieutenants who were encamped there.   In another case, two bodies of troops from the respective armies were separated only by a river, and the officers and soldiers came down to the banks on either side, and held frequent conversations, calling to each other in loud voices across the water.   In this way they succeeded in so far coming to an agreement as to fix upon a time and place for a more formal conference, to be held by commissioners chosen on each side.   This conference was thus held, but each party came to it accompanied by a considerable body of attendants, and these, as might have been anticipated, came into open collision while the discussion was pending; thus the meeting consequently ended in violence and disorder, each party accusing the other of violating the faith which both had plighted.

This slow and undecided mode of warfare between the two vast armies continued for many months without any decisive results. There were skirmishes, struggles, sieges, blockades, and many brief and partial conflicts, but no general and decided battle. Now the advantage seemed on one side, and now on the other. Pompey so hemmed in Cæsar's troops at one period, and so cut off his supplies, that the men were reduced to extreme distress for food. At length they found a kind of root which they dug from the ground, and, after drying and pulverizing it, they made a sort of bread of the powder, which the soldiers were willing to eat rather than either starve or give up the contest. They told Cæsar, in fact, that they would live on the bark of trees rather than abandon his cause. Pompey's soldiers, at one time, coming near to the walls of a town which they occupied, taunted and jeered them on account of their wretched destitution of food. Cæsar's soldiers threw loaves of this bread at them in return, by way of symbol that they were abundantly supplied.

After some time the tide of fortune turned. Cæsar contrived, by a succession of adroit maneuvers and movements, to escape from his toils, and to circumvent and surround Pompey's

forces so as soon to make them suffer destitution
and distress in their turn.   He cut off all communication between them and the country at
large, and turned away the brooks and streams
from flowing through the ground they occupied.
An army of forty or fifty thousand men, with
the immense number of horses and beasts of
burden which accompany them, require very
large supplies of water, and any destitution or
even scarcity of water leads immediately to the
most dreadful consequences.   Pompey's troops
dug wells, but they obtained only very insufficient supplies.   Great numbers of beasts of
burden died, and their decaying bodies so taint-
ed the air as to produce epidemic diseases, which
destroyed many of the troops, and depressed and
disheartened those whom they did not destroy.

During all these operations there was no decisive general battle.   Each one of the great rivals knew very well that his defeat in one general battle would be his utter and irretrievable
ruin.   In a war between two independent nations, a single victory, however complete, seldom terminates the struggle, for the defeated
party has the resources of a whole realm to fall
back upon, which are sometimes called forth
with renewed vigor after experiencing such re-

verses; and then defeat in such cases, even if it be final, does not necessarily involve the ruin of the unsuccessful commander. He may negotiate an honorable peace, and return to his own land in safety; and, if his misfortunes are considered by his countrymen as owing not to any dereliction from his duty as a soldier, but to the influence of adverse circumstances which no human skill or resolution could have controlled, he may spend the remainder of his days in prosperity and honor. The contest, however, between Cæsar and Pompey was not of this character. One or the other of them was a traitor and a usurper—an enemy to his country. The result of a battle would decide which of the two was to stand in this attitude. Victory would legitimize and confirm the authority of one, and make it supreme over the whole civilized world. Defeat was to annihilate the power of the other, and make him a fugitive and a vagabond, without friends, without home, without country. It was a desperate stake; and it is not at all surprising that both parties lingered and hesitated, and postponed the throwing of the die.

At length Pompey, rendered desperate by the urgency of the destitution and distress into

164   J U L I U S   C Æ S A R.   B.C. 48

The armies enter Thessaly.   The plain of Pharsalia

which Cæsar had shut him, made a series of
vigorous and successful attacks upon Cæsar's
lines, by which he broke away in his turn from
his enemy's grasp, and the two armies moved
slowly back into the interior of the country,
hovering in the vicinity of each other, like birds
of prey contending in the air, each continually
striking at the other, and moving onward at the
same time to gain some position of advantage,
or to circumvent the other in such a design.
They passed on in this manner over plains, and
across rivers, and through mountain passes, until at length they reached the heart of Thessaly.   Here at last the armies came to a stand
and fought the final battle.

The place was known then as the plain
of Pharsalia, and the greatness of the contest
which was decided there has immortalized its
name.   Pompey's forces were far more numerous than those of Cæsar, and the advantage in
all the partial contests which had taken place
for some time had been on his side ; he felt, consequently, sure of victory.   He drew up his men
in a line, one flank resting upon the bank of a
river, which protected them from attack on that
side.   From this point, the long line of legions,
drawn up in battle array, extended out upon

B.C. 48.] BATTLE OF PHARSALIA. 165

Roman standard bearers.   Pompey draws up his army

ROMAN STANDARD BEARERS.

the plain, and was terminated at the other extremity by strong squadrons of horse, and bodies
of slingers and archers, so as to give the force
of weapons and the activity of men as great a
range as possible there, in order to prevent Cæsar's being able to outflank and surround them

There was, however, apparently very little
danger of this, for Cæsar, according to his own

story, had but about half as strong a force as
Pompey.   The army of the latter, he says, consisted of nearly fifty thousand men, while his
own number was between twenty and thirty
thousand.   Generals, however, are prone to
magnify the military grandeur of their exploits
by overrating the strength with which they
had to contend, and under-estimating their own.
We are therefore to receive with some distrust
the statements made by Cæsar and his partisans; and as for Pompey's story, the total and
irreparable ruin in which he himself and all who
adhered to him were entirely overwhelmed immediately after the battle, prevented its being
ever told.

In the rear of the plain where Pompey's lines
were extended was the camp from which the
army had been drawn out to prepare for the
battle.   The camp fires of the preceding night
were moldering away, for it was a warm summer morning; the intrenchments were guarded, and the tents, now nearly empty, stood extended in long rows within the inclosure.   In
the midst of them was the magnificent pavilion
of the general, furnished with every imaginable
article of luxury and splendor.   Attendants
were busy here and there, some rearranging

what had been left in disorder by the call to arms by which the troops had been summoned from their places of rest, and others providing refreshments and food for their victorious comrades when they should return from the battle. In Pompey's tent a magnificent entertainment was preparing. The tables were spread with every luxury, the sideboards were loaded with plate, and the whole scene was resplendent with utensils and decorations of silver and gold.

Pompey and all his generals were perfectly certain of victory. In fact, the peace and harmony of their councils in camp had been destroyed for many days by their contentions and disputes about the disposal of the high offices, and the places of profit and power at Rome, which were to come into their hands when Cæsar should have been subdued. The subduing of Cæsar they considered only a question of time; and, as a question of time, it was now reduced to very narrow limits. A few days more, and they were to be masters of the whole Roman empire, and, impatient and greedy, they disputed in anticipation about the division of the spoils.

To make assurance doubly sure, Pompey gave orders that his troops should not advance

to meet the onset of Cæsar's troops on the middle ground between the two armies, but that
they should wait calmly for the attack, and receive the enemy at the posts where they had
themselves been arrayed.

The hour at length arrived, the charge was
sounded by the trumpets, and Cæsar's troops
began to advance with loud shouts and great
impetuosity toward Pompey's lines.   There
was a long and terrible struggle, but the forces
of Pompey began finally to give way.   Notwithstanding the precautions which Pompey had taken to guard and protect the wing of his army
which was extended toward the land, Cæsar
succeeded in turning his flank upon that side
by driving off the cavalry and destroying the
archers and slingers, and he was thus enabled
to throw a strong force upon Pompey's rear
The flight then soon became general, and a
scene of dreadful confusion and slaughter ensued.   The soldiers of Cæsar's army, maddened
with the insane rage which the progress of a
battle never fails to awaken, and now excited
to phrensy by the exultation of success, pressed
on after the affrighted fugitives, who trampled
one upon another, or fell pierced with the weapons of their assailants, filling the air with their

cries of agony and their shrieks of terror. The
horrors of the scene, far from allaying, only excited still more the ferocity of their bloodthirsty
foes, and they pressed steadily and fiercely on,
hour after hour, in their dreadful work of destruction. It was one of those scenes of horror
and woe such as those who have not witnessed
them can not conceive of, and those who have
witnessed can never forget.

When Pompey perceived that all was lost,
he fled from the field in a state of the wildest
excitement and consternation. His troops were
flying in all directions, some toward the camp,
vainly hoping to find refuge there, and others
in various other quarters, wherever they saw
the readiest hope of escape from their merciless
pursuers. Pompey himself fled instinctively
toward the camp. As he passed the guards at
the gate where he entered, he commanded them,
in his agitation and terror, to defend the gate
against the coming enemy, saying that he was
going to the other gates to attend to the defenses
there. He then hurried on, but a full sense of
the helplessness and hopelessness of his condition soon overwhelmed him; he gave up all
thought of defense, and, passing with a sinking
heart through the scene of consternation and

confusion which reigned every where within
the encampment, he sought his own tent, and,
rushing into it, sank down, amid the luxury
and splendor which had been arranged to do
honor to his anticipated victory, in a state of
utter stupefaction and despair.

CHAPTER VIII.

FLIGHT AND DEATH OF POMPEY.

CÆSAR pursued the discomfited and flying bodies of Pompey's army to the camp. They made a brief stand upon the ramparts and at the gates, in a vain and fruitless struggle against the tide of victory which they soon perceived must fully overwhelm them. They gave way continually here and there along the lines of intrenchment, and column after column of Cæsar's followers broke through into the camp. Pompey, hearing from his tent the increasing noise and uproar, was at length aroused from his stupor, and began to summon his faculties to the question what he was to do. At length a party of fugitives, hotly pursued by some of Cæsar's soldiers, broke into his tent. "What!" said Pompey, "into my tent too!" He had been for more than thirty years a victorious general, accustomed to all the deference and respect which boundless wealth, extended and absolute power, and the highest military rank could afford   In the encampments which

he had made, and in the cities which he had
occupied from time to time, he had been the
supreme and unquestioned master, and his tent,
arranged and furnished, as it had always been,
in a style of the utmost magnificence and splendor, had been sacred from all intrusion, and invested with such a dignity that potentates and
princes were impressed when they entered, with
a feeling of deference and awe.   Now, rude
soldiers burst wildly into it, and the air without
was filled with an uproar and confusion, drawing every moment nearer and nearer, and warning the fallen hero that there was no longer any
protection there against the approaching torrent
which was coming on to overwhelm him.

Pompey aroused himself from his stupor,
threw off the military dress which belonged to
his rank and station, and assumed a hasty disguise, in which he hoped he might make his escape from the immediate scene of his calamities.
He mounted a horse and rode out of the camp
at the easiest place of egress in the rear, in company with bodies of troops and guards who were
also flying in confusion, while Cæsar and his
forces on the other side were carrying the intrenchments and forcing their way in.   As soon
as he had thus made his escape from the im-

mediate scene of danger, he dismounted and left
his horse, that he might assume more completely the appearance of a common soldier, and,
with a few attendants who were willing to follow his fallen fortunes, he went on to the eastward, directing his weary steps toward the
shores of the Ægean Sea.

The country through which he was traveling
was Thessaly. Thessaly is a vast amphithea-
ter, surrounded by mountains, from whose sides
streams descend, which, after watering many
fertile valleys and plains, combine to form one
great central river that flows to the eastward,
and after various meanderings, finds its way
into the Ægean Sea through a romantic gap between two mountains, called the Vale of Tempe
—a vale which has been famed in all ages for the
extreme picturesqueness of its scenery, and in
which, in those days, all the charms both of the
most alluring beauty and of the sublimest grandeur seemed to be combined. Pompey followed
the roads leading along the banks of this stream,
weary in body, and harassed and disconsolate
in mind. The news which came to him from
time to time, by the flying parties which were
moving through the country in all directions,
of the entire and overwhelming completeness

of Cæsar's victory, extinguished all remains of
hope, and narrowed down at last the grounds
of his solicitude to the single point of his own
personal safety. He was well aware that he
should be pursued, and, to baffle the efforts
which he knew that his enemies would make
to follow his track, he avoided large towns, and
pressed forward in by-ways and solitudes, bearing as patiently as he was able his increasing
destitution and distress. He reached, at length,
the Vale of Tempe, and there, exhausted with
hunger, thirst, and fatigue, he sat down upon
the bank of the stream to recover by a little
rest strength enough for the remainder of his
weary way. He wished for a drink, but he had
nothing to drink from. And so the mighty potentate, whose tent was full of delicious bever
ages, and cups and goblets of silver and gold,
extended himself down upon the sand at the
margin of the river, and drank the warm water
directly from the stream.

While Pompey was thus anxiously and toil-
somely endeavoring to gain the sea-shore, Cæ
sar was completing his victory over the army
which he had left behind him. When Cæsar
had carried the intrenchments of the camp, and
the army found that there was no longer any

safety for them there, they continued their retreat under the guidance of such generals as remained.   Cæsar thus gained undisputed possession of the camp.   He found every where
the marks of wealth and luxury, and indications of the confident expectation of victory
which the discomfited army had entertained.
The tents of the generals were crowned with
myrtle, the beds were strewed with flowers,
and tables every where were spread for feasts,
with cups and bowls of wine all ready for the
expected revelers.   Cæsar took possession of
the whole, stationed a proper guard to protect
the property, and then pressed forward with his
army in pursuit of the enemy.

Pompey's army made their way to a neighboring rising ground, where they threw up hasty intrenchments to protect themselves for the night
A rivulet ran near the hill, the access to which
they endeavored to secure, in order to obtain
supplies of water.   Cæsar and his forces followed them to this spot.   The day was gone, and it
was too late to attack them.   Cæsar's soldiers,
too, were exhausted with the intense and protracted excitement and exertions which had now
been kept up for many hours in the battle and
in the pursuit, and they needed repose.   **They**

made, however, one effort more. They seized
the avenue of approach to the rivulet, and threw
up a temporary intrenchment to secure it
which intrenchment they protected with a
guard; and then the army retired to rest, leaving their helpless victims to while away the
hours of the night, tormented with thirst, and
overwhelmed with anxiety and despair. · This
could not long be endured. They surrendered
in the morning, and Cæsar found himself in
possession of over twenty thousand prisoners.

In the mean time, Pompey passed on through
the Vale of Tempe toward the sea, regardless of
the beauty and splendor that surrounded him,
and thinking only of his fallen fortunes, and
revolving despairingly in his mind the various
forms in which the final consummation of his
ruin might ultimately come. At length he
reached the sea-shore, and found refuge for the
night in a fisherman's cabin. A small number
of attendants remained with him, some of whom
were slaves. These he now dismissed, directing them to return and surrender themselves to
Cæsar, saying that he was a generous foe, and
that they had nothing to fear from him. His
other attendants he retained, and he made ar
rangements for a boat to take him the next day

along the coast. It was a river boat, and unsuited to the open sea, but it was all that he could obtain.

He arose the next morning at break of day, and embarked in the little vessel, with two or three attendants, and the oarsmen began to row away along the shore. They soon came in sight of a merchant ship just ready to sail. The master of this vessel, it happened, had seen Pompey, and knew his countenance, and he had dreamed, as a famous historian of the times relates, on the night before, that Pompey had come to him in the guise of a simple soldier and in great distress, and that he had received and rescued him. There was nothing extraordinary in such a dream at such a time, as the contest between Cæsar and Pompey, and the approach of the final collision which was to destroy one or the other of them, filled the minds and occupied the conversation of the world. The shipmaster, therefore, having seen and known one of the great rivals in the approaching conflict, would naturally find both his waking and sleeping thoughts dwelling on the subject; and his fancy, in his dreams, might easily picture the scene of his rescuing and saving the fallen hero in the hour of his distress.

However this may be, the shipmaster is said
to have been relating his dream to the seamen
on the deck of his vessel when the boat which
was conveying Pompey came into view.   Pompey himself, having escaped from the land, sup
posed all immediate danger over, not imagining
that seafaring men would recognize him in such
a situation and in such a disguise.   The shipmaster did, however, recognize him.   He was
overwhelmed with grief at seeing him in such
a condition.   With a countenance and with
gestures expressive of earnest surprise and sorrow, he beckoned to Pompey to come on board.
He ordered his own ship's boat to be immediately let down to meet and receive him.   Pompey came on board.   The ship was given up to
his possession, and every possible arrangement
was made to supply his wants, to contribute to
his comfort, and to do him honor.

The vessel conveyed him to Amphipolis, a
city of Macedonia near the sea, and to the northward and eastward of the place where he had
embarked.   When Pompey arrived at the port,
he sent proclamations to the shore, calling upon
the inhabitants to take arms and join his standard.   He did not, however, land, or take any
other measures for carrying these arrangements

into effect. He only waited in the river upon
which Amphipolis stands long enough to receive a supply of money from some of his friends
on the shore, and stores for his voyage, and then
set sail again. Whether he learned that Cæsar was advancing in that direction with a force
too strong for him to encounter, or found that
the people were disinclined to espouse his cause,
or whether the whole movement was a feint to
direct Cæsar's attention to Macedon as the field
of his operations, in order that he might escape
more secretly and safely beyond the sea, can
not now be ascertained.

Pompey's wife Cornelia was on the island of
Lesbos, at Mitylene, near the western coast of
Asia Minor. She was a lady of distinguished
beauty, and of great intellectual superiority and
moral worth. She was extremely well versed
in all the learning of the times, and yet was
entirely free from those peculiarities and airs
which, as her historian says, were often observed in learned ladies in those days. Pompey had married her after the death of Julia,
Cæsar's daughter. They were strongly devoted to each other. Pompey had provided for her
a beautiful retreat on the island of Lesbos,
where she was living in elegance and splendor,

180   JULIUS CÆSAR.   [B.C. 48

Pompey's arrival at Mitylene.   His meeting with Cornelia

beloved for her own intrinsic charms, and highly honored on account of the greatness and fame
of her husband.   Here she had received from
time to time glowing accounts of his success
all exaggerated as they came to her, through
the eager desire of the narrators to give her
pleasure.

From this high elevation of honor and happiness the ill-fated Cornelia suddenly fell, on the
arrival of Pompey's solitary vessel at Mitylene,
bringing as it did, at the same time, both the
first intelligence of her husband's fall, and himself in person, a ruined and homeless fugitive
and wanderer.   The meeting was sad and sorrowful.   Cornelia was overwhelmed at the sud-
denness and violence of the shock which it
brought her, and Pompey lamented anew the
dreadful disaster that he had sustained, at finding how inevitably it must involve his beloved
wife as well as himself in its irreparable ruin.

The pain, however, was not wholly without
some mingling of pleasure.   A husband finds
a strange sense of protection and safety in the
presence and sympathy of an affectionate wife
in the hour of his calamity.   She can, perhaps
do nothing, but her mute and sorrowful con-
sern and pity comfort and reassure him.   Cor

nelia, however, was able to render her husband
some essential aid.   She resolved immediately
to accompany him wherever he should go; and,
by their joint endeavors, a little fleet was gathered, and such supplies as could be hastily obtained, and such attendants and followers as
were willing to share his fate, were taken on
board.   During all this time Pompey would
not go on shore himself, but remained on board
his ship in the harbor.   Perhaps he was afraid
of some treachery or surprise, or perhaps, in
his fallen and hopeless condition, he was unwilling to expose himself to the gaze of those
who had so often seen him in all the splendor
of his former power.

At length, when all was ready, he sailed away
He passed eastward along the Mediterranean,
touching at such ports as he supposed most
likely to favor his cause.   Vague and uncertain, but still alarming rumors that Cæsar was
advancing in pursuit of him met him every
where, and the people of the various provinces
were taking sides, some in his favor and some
against him, the excitement being every where
so great that the utmost caution and circum-
spection were required in all his movements.
Sometimes he was refused permission to land;

at others, his friends were too few to afford him
protection ; and at others still, though the authorities professed friendship, he did not dare to
trust them.　He obtained, however, some supplies of money and some accessions to the number of ships and men under his command, until
at length he had quite a little fleet in his train.
Several men of rank and influence, who had
served under him in the days of his prosperity,
nobly adhered to him now, and formed a sort
of court or council on board his galley, where
they held with their great though fallen commander frequent conversations on the plan which
it was best to pursue.

It was finally decided that it was best to seek
refuge in Egypt.　There seemed to be, in fact,
no alternative.　All the rest of the world was
evidently going over to Cæsar.　Pompey had
been the means, some years before, of restoring
a certain king of Egypt to his throne, and many
of his soldiers had been left in the country, and
remained there still.　It is true that the king
himself had died.　He had left a daughter
named Cleopatra, and also a son, who was at
this time very young.　The name of this youthful prince was Ptolemy.　Ptolemy and Cleopatra had been made by their father joint heirs

to the throne.   But Ptolemy, or, rather, the
ministers and counselors who acted for him and
in his name, had expelled Cleopatra, that they
might govern alone.   Cleopatra had raised an
army in Syria, and was on her way to the fron-
tiers of Egypt to regain possession of what she
deemed her rights.   Ptolemy's ministers had
gone forth to meet her at the head of their own
troops, Ptolemy himself being also with them.
They had reached Pelusium, which is the frontier town between Egypt and Syria on the coast
of the Mediterranean.   Here their armies had
assembled in vast encampments upon the land,
and their galleys and transports were riding at
anchor along the shore of the sea.   Pompey and
his counselors thought that the government of
Ptolemy would receive him as a friend, on account of the services he had rendered to the
young prince's father, forgetting that gratitude
has never a place on the list of political virtues.

Pompey's little squadron made its way slowly
over the waters of the Mediterranean toward
Pelusium and the camp of Ptolemy.   As they
approached the shore, both Pompey himself and
Cornelia felt many anxious forebodings.   A messenger was sent to the land to inform the young
king of Pompey's approach, and to solicit his

protection.　The government of Ptolemy held a
council, and took the subject into consideration

Various opinions were expressed, and various
plans were proposed.　The counsel which was
finally followed was this.　It would be dangerous to receive Pompey, since that would make
Cæsar their enemy.　It would be dangerous to
refuse to receive him, as that would make Pompey their enemy, and, though powerless now, he
might one day be in a condition to seek vengeance.　It was wisest, therefore, to destroy him.
They would invite him to the shore, and kill him
when he landed.　This would please Cæsar;
and Pompey himself, being dead, could never revenge it.　"Dead dogs," as the orator said who
made this atrocious proposal, "do not bite."

An Egyptian, named Achillas, was appointed
to execute the assassination thus decreed.　An
invitation was sent to Pompey to land, accompanied with a promise of protection; and, when
his fleet had approached near enough to the
shore, Achillas took a small party in a boat, and
went out to meet his galley.　The men in this
boat, of course, were armed.

The officers and attendants of Pompey watched all these movements from the deck of his
galley.　They scrutinized every thing that oc-

curred with the closest attention and the greatest anxiety, to see whether the indications de-
noted an honest friendship or intentions of
treachery.   The appearances were not favorable.   Pompey's friends observed that no preparations were making along the shore for receiving him with the honors due, as they thought,
to his rank and station.   The manner, too, in
which the Egyptians seemed to expect him
to land was ominous of evil.   Only a single
insignificant boat for a potentate who recently had commanded half the world!   Then, besides, the friends of Pompey observed that several of the principal galleys of Ptolemy's fleet
were getting up their anchors, and preparing
apparently to be ready to move at a sudden call.
These and other indications appeared much
more like preparations for seizing an enemy
than welcoming a friend.   Cornelia, who, with
her little son, stood upon the deck of Pompey's
galley, watching the scene with a peculiar intensity of solicitude which the hardy soldiers
around her could not have felt, became soon ex-
ceedingly alarmed.   She begged her husband
not to go on shore.   But Pompey decided that
it was now too late to retreat.   He could not
escape from the Egyptian galleys if they had

received orders to intercept him, nor could he
resist violence if violence were intended   To do
any thing like that would evince distrust, and
to appear like putting himself upon his guard
would be to take at once, himself, the position
of an enemy, and invite and justify the hostility
of the Egyptians in return.   As to flight, he
could not hope to escape from the Egyptian galleys if they had received orders to prevent it;
and, besides, if he were determined on attempting an escape, whither should he fly?   The
world was against him.   His triumphant enemy was on his track in full pursuit, with al
the vast powers and resources of the whole Roman empire at his command.   There remained
for Pompey only the last forlorn hope of a refuge
in Egypt, or else, as the sole alternative, a complete and unconditional submission to Cæsar.
His pride would not consent to this, and he determined, therefore, dark as the indications
were, to place himself, without any appearance
of distrust, in Ptolemy's hands, and abide the
issue.

The boat of Achillas approached the galley.
When it touched the side, Achillas and the
other officers on board of it hailed Pompey in
the most respectful manner, giving him the title

of Imperator, the highest title known in the
Roman state.   Achillas addressed Pompey in
Greek.   The Greek was the language of edu-
cated men in all the Eastern countries in those
days.   He told him that the water was too
shallow for his galley to approach nearer to the
shore, and invited him to come on board of his
boat, and he would take him to the beach, where,
as he said, the king was waiting to receive him.

With many anxious forebodings, that were
but ill concealed, Pompey made preparations to
accept the invitation.   He bade his wife farewell, who clung to him as they were about to
part with a gloomy presentiment that they
should never meet again.   Two centurions who
were to accompany Pompey, and two servants,
descended into the boat.   Pompey himself followed, and then the boatmen pushed off from
the galley and made toward the shore.   The
decks of all the vessels in Pompey's little squadron, as well as those of the Egyptian fleet, were
crowded with spectators, and lines of soldiery
and groups of men, all intently watching the
operations of the landing, were scattered along
the shore.

Among the men whom Achillas had provided to aid him in the assassination was an offi-

cer of the Roman army who had formerly served under Pompey. As soon as Pompey was
seated in the boat, he recognized the countenance of this man, and addressed him, saying,
"I think I remember you as having been in former days my fellow-soldier." The man replied
merely by a nod of assent. Feeling somewhat
guilty and self-condemned at the thoughts of
the treachery which he was about to perpetrate,
he was little inclined to renew the recollection
of the days when he was Pompey's friend. In
fact, the whole company in the boat, filled on
the one part with awe in anticipation of the terrible deed which they were soon to commit,
and on the other with a dread suspense and
alarm, were little disposed for conversation,
and Pompey took out a manuscript of an address in Greek which he had prepared to make
to the young king at his approaching interview
with him, and occupied himself in reading it
over. Thus they advanced in a gloomy and
solemn silence, hearing no sound but the dip of
the oars in the water, and the gentle dash of
the waves along the line of the shore.

At length the boat touched the sand, while
Cornelia still stood on the deck of the galley,
watching every movement with great solicitude

and concern. One of the two servants whom
Pompey had taken with him, named Philip, his
favorite personal attendant, rose to assist his
master in landing. He gave Pompey his hand
to aid him in rising from his seat, and at that
moment the Roman officer whom Pompey had
recognized as his fellow-soldier, advanced behind
him and stabbed him in the back. At the same
instant Achillas and the others drew their
swords. Pompey saw that all was lost. He
did not speak, and he uttered no cry of alarm,
though Cornelia's dreadful shriek was so loud
and piercing that it was heard upon the shore.
From the suffering victim himself nothing was
heard but an inarticulate groan extorted by his
agony. He gathered his mantle over his face,
and sank down and died.

Of course, all was now excitement and confusion. As soon as the deed was done, the perpetrators of it retired from the scene, taking
the head of their unhappy victim with them, to
offer to Cæsar as proof that his enemy was re
ally no more. The officers who remained in
the fleet which had brought Pompey to the
coast made all haste to sail away, bearing the
wretched Cornelia with them, utterly distracted with grief and despair, while Philip and his

fellow-servant remained upon the beach, standing bewildered and stupefied over the headless body of their beloved master. Crowds of spectators came in succession to look upon the hideous spectacle a moment in silence, and then to turn, shocked and repelled, away. At length, when the first impulse of excitement had in some measure spent its force, Philip and his comrades so far recovered their composure as to begin to turn their thoughts to the only consolation that was now left to them, that of performing the solemn duties of sepulture. They found the wreck of a fishing boat upon the strand, from which they obtained wood enough for a rude funeral pile. They burned what remained of the mutilated body, and, gathering up the ashes, they put them in an urn and sent them to Cornelia, who afterward buried them at Alba with many bitter tears.

DEATH OF POMPEY.

B.C. 48.] CÆSAR IN EGYPT. 193

Cæsar after the battle of Pharsalia. His clemency.

CHAPTER IX.

CÆSAR IN EGYPT.

CÆSAR surveyed the field of battle after the victory of Pharsalia, not with the feelings of exultation which might have been expected in a victorious general, but with compassion and sorrow for the fallen soldiers whose dead bodies covered the ground. After gazing upon the scene sadly and in silence for a time, he said, "They would have it so," and thus dismissed from his mind all sense of his own responsibility for the consequences which had ensued.

He treated the immense body of prisoners which had fallen into his hands with great clemency, partly from the natural impulses of his disposition, which were always generous and noble, and partly from policy, that he might conciliate them all, officers and soldiers, to acquiescence in his future rule. He then sent back a large portion of his force to Italy, and, taking a body of cavalry from the rest, in order that he might advance with the utmost possible rapidity, he set off through Thessaly and Macedon in pursuit of his fugitive foe.

He had no naval force at his command, and he accordingly kept upon the land. Besides, he wished, by moving through the country at the head of an armed force, to make a demonstration which should put down any attempt that might be made in any quarter to rally or concentrate a force in Pompey's favor. He crossed the Hellespont, and moved down the coast of Asia Minor. There was a great temple consecrated to Diana at Ephesus, which, for its wealth and magnificence, was then the wonder of the world. The authorities who had it in their charge, not aware of Cæsar's approach, had concluded to withdraw the treasures from the temple and loan them to Pompey, to be repaid when he should have regained his power. An assembly was accordingly convened to witness the delivery of the treasures, and take note of their value, which ceremony was to be performed with great formality and parade, when they learned that Cæsar had crossed the Hellespont and was drawing near. The whole proceeding was thus arrested, and the treasures were retained.

Cæsar passed rapidly on through Asia Minor,

B.C. 48.] CÆSAR IN EGYPT. 195

Cæsar in Asia Minor. He sails for Egypt.

examining and comparing, as he advanced, the
vague rumors which were continually coming
in in respect to Pompey's movements. He
learned at length that he had gone to Cyprus;
he presumed that his destination was Egypt,
and he immediately resolved to provide himself
with a fleet, and follow him thither by sea. As
time passed on, and the news of Pompey's defeat and flight, and of Cæsar's triumphant pursuit of him, became generally extended and confirmed, the various powers ruling in all that region of the world abandoned one after another
the hopeless cause, and began to adhere to Cæsar. They offered him such resources and aid
as he might desire. He did not, however, stop
to organize a large fleet or to collect an army.
He depended, like Napoleon, in all the great
movements of his life, not on grandeur of prep
aration, but on celerity of action. He organized at Rhodes a small but very efficient fleet
of ten galleys, and, embarking his best troops
in them, he made sail for the coasts of Egypt.
Pompey had landed at Pelusium, on the eastern frontier, having heard that the young king
and his court were there to meet and resist Cleopatra's invasion. Cæsar, however, with the
characteristic boldness and energy of his char

acter, proceeded directly to Alexandria, the capital.

Egypt was, in those days, an *ally* of the Romans, as the phrase was; that is, the country, though it preserved its independent organization and its forms of royalty, was still united to the Roman people by an intimate league, so as to form an integral part of the great empire. Cæsar, consequently, in appearing there with an armed force, would naturally be received as a friend. He found only the garrison which Ptolemy's government had left in charge of the city. At first the officers of this garrison gave him an outwardly friendly reception, but they soon began to take offense at the air of authority and command which he assumed, and which seemed to them to indicate a spirit of encroachment on the sovereignty of their own king.

Feelings of deeply-seated alienation and animosity sometimes find their outward expression in contests about things intrinsically of very little importance. It was so in this case. The Roman consuls were accustomed to use a certain badge of authority called the *fasces.* It consisted of a bundle of rods, bound around the handle of an ax. Whenever a consul appeared in public, he was preceded by two officers called *lictors*, each of whom carried the fasces as a symbol of the power which was vested in the distinguished personage who followed them.

The Egyptian officers and the people of the city quarreled with Cæsar on account of his moving about among them in his imperial state, accompanied by a life guard, and preceded by the lictors. Contests occurred between his troops and those of the garrison, and many disturbances were created in the streets of the city. Although no serious collision took place, Cæsar thought it prudent to strengthen his force, and he sent back to Europe for additional legions to come to Egypt and join him.

The tidings of Pompey's death came to Cæsar at Alexandria, and with them the head of the murdered man, which was sent by the government of Ptolemy, they supposing that it would be an acceptable gift to Cæsar. Instead of being pleased with it, Cæsar turned from the shocking spectacle in horror. Pompey had been, for many years now gone by, Cæsar's colleague and friend. He had been his son-in-law, and thus had sustained to him a very near and endearing relation. In the contest which had at last unfortunately arisen, Pompey had done no

wrong either to Cæsar or to the government at
Rome.   He was the injured party, so far as
there was a right and a wrong to such a quarrel.   And now, after being hunted through half
the world by his triumphant enemy, he had been
treacherously murdered by men pretending to
receive him as a friend.   The natural sense of
justice, which formed originally so strong a trait
in Cæsar's character, was not yet wholly extinguished.   He could not but feel some remorse at
the thoughts of the long course of violence and
wrong which he had pursued against his old
champion and friend, and which had led at last
to so dreadful an end.   Instead of being pleased with the horrid trophy which the Egyptians
sent him, he mourned the death of his great rival with sincere and unaffected grief, and was
filled with indignation against his murderers.

Pompey had a signet ring upon his finger at
the time of his assassination, which was taken
off by the Egyptian officers and carried away
to Ptolemy, together with the other articles of
value which had been found upon his person
Ptolemy sent this seal to Cæsar to complete the
proof that its possessor was no more.   Cæsar received *this* memorial with eager though mourn-
ful pleasure, and he preserved it with great

care. And in many ways, during all the remainder of his life, he manifested every outward
indication of cherishing the highest respect for
Pompey's memory There stands to the present day, among the ruins of Alexandria, a beautiful column, about one hundred feet high, which
has been known in all modern times as POMPEY'S
PILLAR. It is formed of stone, and is in three

POMPEY'S PILLAR.

200 JULIUS CÆSAR. [B.C. 48.

Origin of Pompey's Pillar.   Surrender of Pompey's officers

parts. One stone forms the pedestal, another
the shaft, and a third the capital. The beauty
of this column, the perfection of its workman-
ship, which still continues in excellent preservation, and its antiquity, so great that all distinct record of its origin is lost, have combined
to make it for many ages the wonder and admiration of mankind. Although no history of
its origin has come down to us, a tradition has
descended that Cæsar built it during his residence in Egypt, to commemorate the name of
Pompey; but whether it was his own victory
over Pompey, or Pompey's own character and
military fame which the structure was intended
to signalize to mankind, can not now be known.
There is even some doubt whether it was erected by Cæsar at all.

While Cæsar was in Alexandria, many of
Pompey's officers, now that their master was
dead, and there was no longer any possibility
of their rallying again under his guidance and
command, came in and surrendered themselves
to him. He received them with great kindness,
and, instead of visiting them with any penal-
ties for having fought against him, he honored
the fidelity and bravery they had evinced in the
service of their own former master. Cæsar had,

in fact, shown the same generosity to the soldiers of Pompey's army that he had taken prisoners at the battle of Pharsalia.   At the close
of the battle, he issued orders that each one of
his soldiers should have permission to *save* one
of the enemy.   Nothing could more strikingly
exemplify both the generosity and the tact that
marked the great conqueror's character than
this incident.   The hatred and revenge which
had animated his victorious soldiery in the battle
and in the pursuit, were changed immediately
by the permission to compassion and good will.
The ferocious soldiers turned at once from the
pleasure of hunting their discomfited enemies
to death, to that of protecting and defending
them; and the way was prepared for their being
received into his service, and incorporated with
the rest of his army as friends and brothers.

Cæsar soon found himself in so strong a position at Alexandria, that he determined to exercise his authority as Roman consul to settle
the dispute in respect to the succession of the
Egyptian crown.   There was no difficulty in
finding pretexts for interfering in the affairs of
Egypt.   In the first place, there was, as he con-
tended, great anarchy and confusion at Alexandria, people taking different sides in the con-

troversy with such fierceness as to render it impossible that good government and public order should be restored until this great question was settled.   He also claimed a debt due from the Egyptian government, which Photinus, Ptolemy's minister at Alexandria, was very dilatory in paying.   This led to animosities and disputes; and, finally, Cæsar found, or pretended to find, evidence that Photinus was forming plots against his life.   At length Cæsar determined on taking decided action.   He sent orders both to Ptolemy and to Cleopatra to disband their forces, to repair to Alexandria, and lay their respective claims before him for his adjudication.

Cleopatra complied with this summons, and returned to Egypt with a view to submitting her case to Cæsar's arbitration.   Ptolemy determined to resist.   He advanced toward Egypt, but it was at the head of his army, and with a determination to drive Cæsar and all his Roman followers away.

When Cleopatra arrived, she found that the avenues of approach to Cæsar's quarters were all in possession of her enemies, so that, in attempting to join him, she incurred danger of falling into their hands as a prisoner.   She resorted to a stratagem, as the story is, to gain a

secret admission.   They rolled her up in a sort
of bale of bedding or carpeting, and she was
carried in in this way on the back of a man,
through the guards, who might otherwise have
intercepted her.   Cæsar was very much pleased
with this device, and with the successful result
of it.   Cleopatra, too, was young and beautiful,
and Cæsar immediately conceived a strong but
guilty attachment to her, which she readily returned.   Cæsar espoused her cause, and decided
that she and Ptolemy should jointly occupy the
throne.

Ptolemy and his partisans were determined
not to submit to this award.   The consequence
was, a violent and protracted war.   Ptolemy
was not only incensed at being deprived of what
he considered his just right to the realm, he was
also half distracted at the thought of his sister's
disgraceful connection with Cæsar.   His excitement and distress, and the exertions and efforts to which they aroused him, awakened a
strong sympathy in his cause among the people,
and Cæsar found himself involved in a very serious contest, in which his own life was brought
repeatedly into the most imminent danger, and
which seriously threatened the total destruction
of his power.   He, however, braved all the dif-

ficulty and dangers, and recklessly persisted in
the course he had taken, under the influence of
the infatuation in which his attachment to Cleopatra held him, as by a spell.

The war in which Cæsar was thus involved
by his efforts to give Cleopatra a seat with her
brother on the Egyptian throne, is called in history the Alexandrine war. It was marked by
many strange and romantic incidents. There
was a light-house, called the Pharos, on a small
island opposite the harbor of Alexandria, and it
was so famed, both on account of the great magnificence of the edifice itself, and also on account
of its position at the entrance to the greatest
commercial port in the world, that it has given
its name, as a generic appellation, to all other
structures of the kind—any light-house being
now called a Pharos, just as any serious difficulty is called a Gordian knot. The Pharos
was a lofty tower—the accounts say that it was
five hundred feet in height, which would be an
enormous elevation for such a structure—and
in a lantern at the top a brilliant light was kept
constantly burning, which could be seen over
the water for a hundred miles. The tower was
built in several successive stories, each being
ornamented with balustrades, galleries. and col

umns, so that the splendor of the architecture
by day rivaled the brilliancy of the radiation
which beamed from the summit by night.   Far
and wide over the stormy waters of the Mediterranean this meteor glowed, inviting and guid-
ing the mariners in; and both its welcome and
its guidance were doubly prized in those ancient
days, when there was neither compass nor sex-
tant on which they could rely.   In the course
of the contest with the Egyptians, Cæsar took
possession of the Pharos, and of the island on
which it stood; and as the Pharos was then
regarded as one of the seven wonders of the
world, the fame of the exploit, though it was
probably nothing remarkable in a military point
of view, spread rapidly throughout the world.

And yet, though the capture of a light-house
was no very extraordinary conquest, in the
course of the contests on the harbor which were
connected with it Cæsar had a very narrow
escape from death.   In all such struggles he was
accustomed always to take personally his full
share of the exposure and the danger.   This
resulted in part from the natural impetuosity
and ardor of his character, which were always
aroused to double intensity of action by the excitement of battle, and partly from the ideas

of the military duty of a commander which prevailed in those days. There was besides, in
this case, an additional inducement to acquire
the glory of extraordinary exploits, in Cæsar's
desire to be the object of Cleopatra's admiration, who watched all his movements, and who
was doubly pleased with his prowess and bravery, since she saw that they were exercised for
her sake and in her cause.

The Pharos was built upon an island, which
was connected by a pier or bridge with the main
land. In the course of the attack upon this
bridge, Cæsar, with a party of his followers, got
driven back and hemmed in by a body of the
enemy that surrounded them, in such a place
that the only mode of escape seemed to be by a
boat, which might take them to a neighboring
galley. They began, therefore, all to crowd into
the boat in confusion, and so overloaded it that
it was obviously in imminent danger of being
upset or of sinking. The upsetting or sinking
of an overloaded boat brings almost certain destruction upon most of the passengers, whether
swimmers or not, as they seize each other in
their terror, and go down inextricably entangled
together, each held by the others in the convulsive grasp with which drowning men always

cling to whatever is within their reach. Cæsar, anticipating this danger, leaped over into the sea and swam to the ship. He had some papers in his hand at the time—plans, perhaps, of the works which he was assailing. These he held above the water with his left hand, while he swam with the right. And to save his purple cloak or mantle, the emblem of his imperial dignity, which he supposed the enemy would eagerly seek to obtain as a trophy, he seized it by a corner between his teeth, and drew it after him through the water as he swam toward the galley. The boat which he thus escaped from soon after went down, with all on board.

During the progress of this Alexandrine war one great disaster occurred, which has given to the contest a most melancholy celebrity in all subsequent ages : this disaster was the destruction of the Alexandrian library. The Egyptians were celebrated for their learning, and, under the munificent patronage of some of their kings, the learned men of Alexandria had made an enormous collection of writings, which were inscribed, as was the custom in those days, on parchment rolls. The number of the rolls or volumes was said to be seven hundred thousand; and when we conside that each one was writ-

ten with great care, in beautiful characters, with
a pen, and at a vast expense, it is not surprising
that the collection was the admiration of the
world.   In fact, the whole body of ancient literature was there recorded.   Cæsar set fire to some
Egyptian galleys, which lay so near the shore
that the wind blew the sparks and flames upon the
buildings on the quay.   The fire spread among
the palaces and other magnificent edifices of that
part of the city, and one of the great buildings
in which the library was stored was reached and
destroyed.   There was no other such collection
in the world; and the consequence of this calamity has been, that it is only detached and insu-
lated fragments of ancient literature and science
that have come down to our times.   The world
will never cease to mourn the irreparable loss.

Notwithstanding the various untoward incidents which attended the war in Alexandria
during its progress, Cæsar, as usual, conquered
in the end.   The young king Ptolemy was defeated, and, in attempting to make his escape
across a branch of the Nile, he was drowned.
Cæsar then finally settled the kingdom upon
Cleopatra and a younger brother, and, after remaining for some time longer in Egypt, he set
out on his return to Rome.

CLEOPATRA'S BARGE.

The subsequent adventures of Cleopatra were
so romantic as to have given her name a very
wide celebrity.   The lives of the virtuous pass
smoothly and happily away, but the tale, when
told to others, possesses but little interest or attraction ; while those of the wicked, whose days
are spent in wretchedness and despair, and are
thus full of misery to the actors themselves, afford to the rest of mankind a high degree of
pleasure, from the dramatic interest of the story.

Cleopatra led a life of splendid sin, and, of
course, of splendid misery.   She visited Cæsar
in Rome after his return thither.   Cæsar received her magnificently, and paid her all possible honors ; but the people of Rome regarded
her with strong reprobation.   When her young
brother, whom Cæsar had made her partner on
the throne, was old enough to claim his share,
she poisoned him.   After Cæsar's death, she
went from Alexandria to Syria to meet Antony, one of Cæsar's successors, in a galley or
barge, which was so rich, so splendid, so magnificently furnished and adorned, that it was
famed throughout the world as Cleopatra's
barge.   A great many beautiful vessels have
since been called by the same name.   Cleopatra connected herself with Antony, who became

infatuated with her beauty and her various
charms as Cæsar had been.　After a great variety of romantic adventures, Antony was defeated in battle by his great rival Octavius, and,
supposing that he had been betrayed by Cleopatra, he pursued her to Egypt, intending to
kill her.　She hid herself in a sepulcher, spreading a report that she had committed suicide,
and then Antony stabbed himself in a fit of
remorse and despair.　Before he died, he learned that Cleopatra was alive, and he caused himself to be carried into her presence and died in
her arms.　Cleopatra then fell into the hands
of Octavius, who intended to carry her to Rome
to grace his triumph.　To save herself from
this humiliation, and weary with a life which,
full of sin as it had been, was a constant series
of sufferings, she determined to die.　A servant
brought in an asp for her, concealed in a vase
of flowers, at a great banquet.　She laid the
poisonous reptile on her naked arm, and died
immediately of the bite which it inflicted

Chapter X.

Cæsar Imperator.

ALTHOUGH Pompey himself had been killed, and the army under his immediate command entirely annihilated, Cæsar did not find that the empire was yet completely submissive to his sway. As the tidings of his conquests spread over the vast and distant regions which were under the Roman rule—although the story itself of his exploits might have been exaggerated—the impression produced by his power lost something of its strength, as men generally have little dread of remote danger. While he was in Egypt, there were three great concentrations of power formed against him in other quarters of the globe: in Asia Minor, in Africa, and in Spain. In putting down these three great and formidable arrays of opposition, Cæsar made an exhibition to the world of that astonishing promptness and celerity of military action on which his fame as a general so much depends. He went first to Asia Minor, and fought a great and decisive battle there, in

a manner so sudden and unexpected to the
forces that opposed him that they found themselves defeated almost before they suspected that
their enemy was near.   It was in reference to
this battle that he wrote the inscription for the
banner, "*Veni, vidi, vici*."   The words may be
rendered in English, "I came, looked, and conquered," though the peculiar force of the expression, as well as the alliteration, is lost in
any attempt to translate it.

In the mean time, Cæsar's prosperity and
success had greatly strengthened his cause at
Rome.   Rome was supported in a great measure by the contributions brought home from the
provinces by the various military heroes who
were sent out to govern them ; and, of course,
the greater and more successful was the conqueror, the better was he qualified for stations
of highest authority in the estimation of the
inhabitants of the city.   They made Cæsar
dictator even while he was away, and appointed
Mark Antony his master of horse.   This was
the same Antony whom we have already mentioned as having been connected with Cleopatra
after Cæsar's death.   Rome, in fact, was filled
with the fame of Cæsar's exploits, and, as he
crossed the Adriatic and advanced toward the

city, he found himself the object of universal
admiration and applause.

But he could not yet be contented to estab-
lish himself quietly at Rome.   There was a
large force organized against him in Africa under Cato, a stern and indomitable man, who had
long been an enemy to Cæsar, and who now
considered him as a usurper and an enemy of
the republic, and was determined to resist him
to the last extremity.   There was also a large
force assembled in Spain under the command
of two sons of Pompey, in whose case the ordinary political hostility of contending partisans
was rendered doubly intense and bitter by their
desire to avenge their father's cruel fate.   Cæsar
determined first to go to Africa, and then, after
disposing of Cato's resistance, to cross the Mediterranean into Spain.

Before he could set out, however, on these
expeditions, he was involved in very serious
difficulties for a time, on account of a great discontent which prevailed in his army, and which
ended at last in open mutiny.   The soldiers
complained that they had not received the rewards and honors which Cæsar had promised
them.   Some claimed offices, others money,
others lands, which, as they maintained, they

had been led to expect would be conferred upon them at the end of the campaign. The fact undoubtedly was, that, elated with their success, and intoxicated with the spectacle of the boundless influence and power which their general so obviously wielded at Rome, they formed expectations and hopes for themselves altogether too wild and unreasonable to be realized by soldiers; for soldiers, however much they may be flattered by their generals in going into battle, or praised in the mass in official dispatches, are after all but slaves, and slaves, too, of the very humblest caste and character.

The famous tenth legion, Cæsar's favorite corps, took the most active part in fomenting these discontents, as might naturally have been expected, since the attentions and the praises which he had bestowed upon them, though at first they tended to awaken their ambition, and to inspire them with redoubled ardor and courage, ended, as such favoritism always does, in making them vain, self-important, and unreasonable. Led on thus by the tenth legion, the whole army mutinied. They broke up the camp where they had been stationed at some distance beyond the walls of Rome, and marched toward the city. Soldiers in a mutiny, even though headed by their subaltern officers, are very little under command; and these Roman troops, feeling released from their usual restraints, committed various excesses on the way, terrifying the inhabitants and spreading universal alarm. The people of the city were thrown into utter consternation at the approach of the vast horde, which was coming like a terrible avalanche to descend upon them.

The army expected some signs of resistance at the gates, which, if offered, they were prepared to encounter and overcome. Their plan was, after entering the city, to seek Cæsar and demand their discharge from his service. They knew that he was under the necessity of immediately making a campaign in Africa, and that, of course, he could not possibly, as they supposed, dispense with them. He would, consequently, if they asked their discharge, beg them to remain, and, to induce them to do it, would comply with all their expectations and desires.

Such was their plan. To tender, however, a resignation of an office as a means of bringing an opposite party to terms, is always a very hazardous experiment. We easily overrate the estimation in which our own services are held

taking what is said to us in kindness or cour-
tesy by friends as the sober and deliberate judgment of the public; and thus it often happens
that persons who in such case offer to resign,
are astonished to find their resignations readily
accepted.

When Cæsar's mutineers arrived at the gates,
they found, instead of opposition, only orders
from Cæsar, by which they were directed to
leave all their arms except their swords, and
march into the city. They obeyed. They
were then directed to go to the Campus Martius, a vast parade ground situated within the
walls, and to await Cæsar's orders there.*

Cæsar met them in the Campus Martius,
and demanded why they had left their encampment without orders and come to the city.
They stated in reply, as they had previously
planned to do, that they wished to be discharged
from the public service. To their great astonishment, Cæsar seemed to consider this request
as nothing at all extraordinary, but promised,
on the other hand, very readily to grant it   He
said that they should be at once discharged, and
should receive faithfully all the rewards which
had been promised them at the close of the war

* See map of the city of Rome, fronting the first page.

for their long and arduous services.   At the
same time, he expressed his deep regret that,
to obtain what he was perfectly willing and
ready at any time to grant, they should have
so far forgotten their duties as Romans, and
violated the discipline which should always be
held absolutely sacred by every soldier.   He
particularly regretted that the tenth legion, on
which he had been long accustomed so implicitly to rely, should have taken a part in such transactions.

In making this address, Cæsar assumed a
kind and considerate, and even respectful tone
toward his men, calling them *Quirites* instead
of soldiers—an honorary mode of appellation,
which recognized them as constituent members
of the Roman commonwealth.   The effect of
the whole transaction was what might have
been anticipated.   A universal desire was
awakened throughout the whole army to return
to their duty.   They sent deputations to Cæsar,
begging not to be taken at their word, but to be
retained in the service, and allowed to accompany him to Africa.   After much hesitation
and delay, Cæsar consented to receive them
again, all excepting the tenth legion, who, he
said, had now irrevocably lost his confidence

and regard.   It is a striking illustration of the strength of the attachment which bound Cæsar's soldiers to their commander, that the tenth legion *would not* be discharged, after all.   They followed Cæsar of their own accord into Africa, earnestly entreating him again and again to receive them.   He finally did receive them in detachments, which he incorporated with the rest of his army, or sent on distant service, but he would never organize them as the tenth legion again.

It was now early in the winter, a stormy season for crossing the Mediterranean Sea. Cæsar, however, set off from Rome immediately, proceeded south to Sicily, and encamped on the sea-shore there till the fleet was ready to convey his forces to Africa.   The usual fortune attended him in the African campaigns   His fleet was exposed to imminent dangers in crossing the sea, but, in consequence of the extreme deliberation and skill with which his arrangements were made, he escaped them all.   He overcame one after another of the military difficulties which were in his way in Africa.   His army endured, in the depth of winter, great exposures and fatigues, and they had to encounter a large hostile force under the charge of Cato

They were, however, successful in every undertaking.   Cato retreated at last to the city of
Utica, where he shut himself up with the remains of his army; but finding, at length, when
Cæsar drew near, that there was no hope or possibility of making good his defense, and as his
stern and indomitable spirit could not endure
the thought of submission to one whom he cor
sidered as an enemy to his country and a traito,
he resolved upon a very effectual mode of escaping from his conqueror's power.

He feigned to abandon all hope of defending
the city, and began to make arrangements to
facilitate the escape of his soldiers over the sea.
He collected the vessels in the harbor, and allowed all to embark who were willing to take
the risks of the stormy water.   He took, apparently, great interest in the embarkations, and,
when evening came on, he sent repeatedly down
to the sea-side to inquire about the state of the
wind and the progress of the operations.   At
length he retired to his apartment, and, when
all was quiet in the house, he lay down upor
his bed and stabbed himself with his sword
He fell from the bed by the blow, or else from
the effect of some convulsive motion which the
penetrating steel occasioned.   His son and serv

ants, hearing the fall, came rushing into the room, raised him from the floor, and attempted to bind up and stanch the wound. Cato would not permit them to do it. He resisted them violently as soon as he was conscious of what they intended. Finding that a struggle would only aggravate the horrors of the scene, and even hasten its termination, they left the bleeding hero to his fate, and in a few minutes he died.

The character of Cato, and the circumstances under which his suicide was committed, make it, on the whole, the most conspicuous act of suicide which history records; and the events which followed show in an equally conspicuous manner the extreme folly of the deed. In respect to its wickedness, Cato, not having had the light of Christianity before him, is to be leniently judged. As to the folly of the deed, however, he is to be held strictly accountable. If he had lived and yielded to his conqueror, as he might have done gracefully and without dishonor, since all his means of resistance were exhausted, Cæsar would have treated him with generosity and respect, and would have taken him to Rome; and as within a year or two of this time Cæsar himself was no more, Cato's vast influence and power might have been, and un-

doubtedly would have been, called most effectually into action for the benefit of his country.
If any one, in defending Cato, should say he
could not foresee this, we reply, he *could* have
foreseen it; not the precise events, indeed, which
occurred, but he could have foreseen that vast
changes must take place, and new aspects of
affairs arise, in which his powers would be called
into requisition.   We can *always* foresee in the
midst of any storm, however dark and gloomy,
that clear skies will certainly sooner or later
come again; and this is just as true metaphori-
cally in respect to the vicissitudes of human
life, as it is literally in regard to the ordinary
phenomena of the skies.

From Africa Cæsar returned to Rome, and
from Rome he went to subdue the resistance
which was offered by the sons of Pompey in
Spain.   He was equally successful here.   The
oldest son was wounded in battle, and was carried off from the field upon a litter faint and
almost dying.   He recovered in some degree,
and, finding escape from the eager pursuit of
Cæsar's soldiers impossible, he concealed himself in a cave, where he lingered for a little
time in destitution and misery.   He was discovered at las⁺; his head was cut off by his

captors and sent to Cæsar, as his father's had
been.   The younger son succeeded in escaping,
but he became a wretched fugitive and outlaw,
and all manifestations of resistance to Cæsar's
sway disappeared from Spain.   The conqueror
returned to Rome the undisputed master of the
whole Roman world.

Then came his triumphs.   Triumphs were
great celebrations, by which military heroes in
the days of the Roman commonwealth signalized their victories on their return to the city
Cæsar's triumphs were four, one for each of his
four great successful campaigns, viz., in Egypt,
in Asia Minor, in Africa, and in Spain.   Each
was celebrated on a separate day, and there was
an interval of several days between them, to
magnify their importance, and swell the general
interest which they excited among the vast
population of the city.   On one of these days,
the triumphal car in which Cæsar rode, which
was most magnificently adorned, broke down on
the way, and Cæsar was nearly thrown out of
it by the shock.   The immense train of cars,
horses, elephants, flags, banners, captives, and
trophies which formed the splendid procession
was all stopped by the accident, and a considerable delay ensued.   Night came on, in fact

THE ELEPHANTS MADE TORCH-BEARERS.

before the column could again be put in motion
to enter the city, and then Cæsar, whose genius
was never more strikingly shown than when he
had opportunity to turn a calamity to advantage, conceived the idea of employing the forty
elephants of the train as torch-bearers; the
long procession accordingly advanced through
the streets and ascended to the Capitol, lighted
by the great blazing flambeaus which the sagacious and docile beasts were easily taught to
bear, each elephant holding one in his proboscis,
and waving it above the crowd around him.

In these triumphal processions, every thing
was borne in exhibition which could serve as a
symbol of the conquered country or a trophy of
victory. Flags and banners taken from the
enemy; vessels of gold and silver, and other
treasures, loaded in vans; wretched captives
conveyed in open carriages or marching sor-
rowfully on foot, and destined, some of them,
to public execution when the ceremony of the
triumph was ended; displays of arms, and im-
plements, and dresses, and all else which might
serve to give the Roman crowd an idea of the
customs and usages of the remote and conquered
nations; the animals they used, caparisoned in
the manner in which they used them: these,

and a thousand other trophies and emblems,
were brought into the line to excite the admira·
tion of the crowd, and to add to the gorgeous·
ness of the spectacle.   In fact, it was always a
great object of solicitude and exertion with all
the Roman generals, when on distant a⁻ l dangerous expeditions, to possess thems⟨ ⟩es of
every possible prize in the progress of t⟩ ir campaign which could aid in adding splen ⟨ ⟩r to the
triumph which was to signalize its end.

In these triumphs of Cæsar, a young sister
of Cleopatra was in the line of the Egyptian
procession.   In that devoted to Asia Minor was
a great banner containing the words already re·
ferred to, VENI, VIDI, VICI.   There were great
paintings, too, borne aloft, representing battles
and other striking scenes.   Of course, all Rome
was in the highest state of excitement during
the days of the exhibition of this pageantry.
The whole surrounding country flocked to the
capital to witness it, and Cæsar's greatness and
glory were signalized in the most conspicuous
manner to all mankind

After these tr'umphs, a series of splendid
public entertainments were given, over twenty
thousand tables having been spread for the pop
ulace of the city   Shows of every possible char

acter and variety were exhibited. There were
dramatic plays, and equestrian performances in
the circus, and gladiatorial combats, and battles
with wild beasts, and dances, and chariot races,
and every other imaginable amusement which
could be devised and carried into effect to gratify a population highly cultivated in all the arts
of life, but barbarous and cruel in heart and character. Some of the accounts which have come
down to us of the magnificence of the scale on
which these entertainments were conducted
are absolutely incredible. It is said, for example, that an immense basin was constructed
near the Tiber, large enough to contain two
fleets of galleys, which had on board two thousand rowers each, and one thousand fighting
men. These fleets were then manned with
captives, the one with Asiatics and the other
with Egyptians, and when all was ready, they
were compelled to fight a real battle for the
amusement of the spectators which thronged
the shores, until vast numbers were killed, and
the waters of the lake were dyed with blood.
It is also said that the whole Forum, and some
of the great streets in the neighborhood where
the principal gladiatorial shows were held, were
covered with silken awnings to protect the vast

crowds of spectators from the sun, and thousands of tents were erected to accommodate the people from the surrounding country, whom th buildings of the city could not contain.

All open opposition to Cæsar's power and dominion now entirely disappeared. Even the Senate vied with the people in rendering him every possible honor. The supreme power had been hitherto lodged in the hands of two consuls, chosen annually, and the Roman people had been extremely jealous of any distinction for any one, higher than that of an *elective annual office*, with a return to private life again when the brief period should have expired. They now, however, made Cæsar, in the first place, consul for ten years, and then Perpetual Dictator. They conferred upon him the title of the Father of his Country. The name of the month in which he was born was changed to Julius, from his prænomen, and we still retain the name. He was made, also, commander-in-chief of all the armies of the commonwealth, the title to which vast military power was expressed in the Latin language by the word IMPERATOR.

Cæsar was highly elated with all these substantial proofs of the greatness and glory to which he had attained, and was also very evi-

B.C. 47.] CÆSAR IMPERATOR 231

Statues of Cæsar. His plans of internal improvement.

dently gratified with smaller, but equally expressive proofs of the general regard. Statues representing his person were placed in the public edifices, and borne in processions like those of the gods. Conspicuous and splendidly ornamented seats were constructed for him in all the places of public assembly, and on these he sat to listen to debates or witness spectacles, as if he were upon a throne. He had, either by his influence or by his direct power, the control of all the appointments to office, and was, in fact, in every thing but the name, a sovereign and an absolute king.

He began now to form great schemes of internal improvement for the general benefit of the empire. He wished to increase still more the great obligations which the Roman people were under to him for what he had already done. They really were under vast obligations to him; for, considering Rome as a community which was to subsist by governing the world, Cæsar had immensely enlarged the means of its subsistence by establishing its sway every where, and providing for an incalculable increase of its revenues from the tribute and the taxation of conquered provinces and kingdoms. Since this work of conquest was now completed, he turned his attention to the internal affairs of the empire, and made many improvements in the system of administration, looking carefully into every thing, and introducing every where those exact and systematic principles which such a mind as his seeks instinctively in every thing over which it has any control.

One great change which he effected continues in perfect operation throughout Europe to the present day.   It related to the division of time. The system of months in use in his day corresponded so imperfectly with the annual circuit of the sun, that the months were moving continually along the year in such a manner that the winter months came at length in the summer, and the summer months in the winter. This led to great practical inconveniences; for whenever, for example, any thing was required by law to be done in certain months, intending to have them done in the summer, and the specified month came at length to be a winter month, the law would require the thing to be done in exactly the wrong season.   Cæsar remedied all this by adopting a new system of months, which should give three hundred and sixty-five days to the year for three years, and three hundred and sixty-six for the fourth; and

so exact was the system which he thus introduced, that it went on unchanged for sixteen
centuries. The months were then found to be
eleven days out of the way, when a new cor
rection was introduced,* and it will now go
on three thousand years before the error will
amount to a single day. Cæsar employed a
Greek astronomer to arrange the system that
he adopted ; and it was in part on account of
the improvement which he thus effected that
one of the months, as has already been mentioned, was called July. Its name before was
Quintilis.

Cæsar formed a great many other vast and
magnificent schemes. He planned public buildings for the city, which were going to exceed in
magnitude and splendor all the edifices of the
world. He commenced the collection of vast
libraries, formed plans for draining the Pontine
Marshes, for bringing great supplies of water
into the city by an aqueduct, for cutting a new
passage for the Tiber from Rome to the sea,
and making an enormous artificial harbor at its
mouth. He was going to make a road along
the Apennines, and cut a canal through the

* By Pope Gregory XIII. at the time of the change from
the old style to the new

Cæsar collects the means to carry out his vast schemes.

Isthmus of Corinth, and construct other vast
works, which were to make Rome the center of
the commerce of the world.   In a word, his
head was filled with the grandest schemes, and
he was gathering around him all the means and
resources necessary for the execution of them.

B.C. 44.]   THE CONSPIRACY.   235

Jealousies awakened by Cæsar's power.   The Roman Constitution

CHAPTER XI.

THE CONSPIRACY.

CÆSAR'S greatness and glory came at last to a very sudden and violent end. He was assassinated. All the attendant circumstances of this deed, too, were of the most extraordinary character, and thus the dramatic interest which adorns all parts of the great conqueror's history marks strikingly its end.

His prosperity and power awakened, of course, a secret jealousy and ill will. Those who were disappointed in their expectations of his favor murmured. Others, who had once been his rivals, hated him for having triumphed over them. Then there was a stern spirit of democracy, too, among certain classes of the citizens of Rome which could not brook a master. It is true that the sovereign power in the Roman commonwealth had never been shared by all the inhabitants. It was only in certain privileged classes that the sovereignty was vested; but among these the functions of government were divided and distributed in such a way as to

balance one interest against another, and to give
all their proper share of influence and authority.
Terrible struggles and conflicts often occurred
among these various sections of society, as one
or another attempted from time to time to en-
croach upon the rights or privileges of the rest.
These struggles, however, ended usually in at
last restoring again the equilibrium which had
been disturbed. No one power could ever gain
the entire ascendency; and thus, as all *monarch-
ism* seemed excluded from their system, they
called it a republic. Cæsar, however, had now
concentrated in himself all the principal elements
of power, and there began to be suspicions that
he wished to make himself in name and openly,
as well as secretly and in fact, a king.

The Romans abhorred the very name of king.
They had had kings in the early periods of their
history, but they made themselves odious by
their pride and their oppressions, and the people
had deposed and expelled them. The modern
nations of Europe have several times performed
the same exploit, but they have generally felt
unprotected and ill at ease without a personal
sovereign over them, and have accordingly, in
most cases, after a few years, restored some
branch of the expelled dynasty to the throne

The Romans were more persevering and firm.
They had managed their empire now for five
hundred years as a republic, and though they
had had internal dissensions, conflicts, and quarrels without end, had persisted so firmly and
unanimously in their detestation of all regal
authority, that no one of the long line of ambitious and powerful statesmen, generals, or conquerors by which the history of the empire had
been signalized, had ever dared to aspire to the
name of king.

There began, however, soon to appear some
indications that Cæsar, who certainly now possessed regal power, would like the regal name.
Ambitious men, in such cases, do not directly
assume themselves the titles and symbols of
royalty.   Others make the claim for them, while
they faintly disavow it, till they have opportunity to see what effect the idea produces on
the public mind.   The following incidents occurred which it was thought indicated such a
design on the part of Cæsar.

There were in some of the public buildings
certain statues of kings; or it must be understood that the Roman dislike to kings was only
a dislike to having kingly authority exercised
over themselves.   They respected and some-

times admired the kings of other countries, and
honored their exploits, and made statues to commemorate their fame. They were willing that
kings should reign elsewhere, so long as there
were no king of Rome. The American feeling
at the present day is much the same. If the
Queen of England were to make a progress
through this country, she would receive, perhaps, as many and as striking marks of attention and honor as would be rendered to her in
her own realm. We venerate the antiquity of
her royal line; we admire the efficiency of her
government and the sublime grandeur of her
empire, and have as high an idea as any, of the
powers and prerogatives of her crown—and these
feelings would show themselves most abundantly on any proper occasion. We are willing,
nay, ' h that she should continue to reign over
Englishmen; and yet, after all, it would take
some millions of bay aets to place a queen se-
curely upon a throne over this land.

Regal power was accordingly, in the ab-
stract, looked up to at Rome, as it is elsewhere,
with great respect; and it was, in fact, all the
more tempting as an object of ambition, from the
determination felt by the people that it should
not be exercised there. There were, according-

ly, statues of kings at Rome. Cæsar placed
his own statue among them. Some approved,
others murmured.

There was a public theater in the city, where
the officers of the government were accustomed to sit in honorable seats prepared expressly
for them, those of the Senate being higher
and more distinguished than the rest. Cæsar
had a seat prepared for himself there, similar in form to a throne, and adorned it magnificently with gilding and ornaments of gold,
which gave it the entire pre-eminence over all
the other seats.

He had a similar throne placed in the senate
chamber, to be occupied by himself when attending there, like the throne of the King of England in the House of Lords.

He held, moreover, a great many public celebrations and triumphs in the city in commem-
oration of his exploits and honors; and, on one
of these occasions, it was arranged that the
Senate were to come to him at a temple in a
body, and announce to him certain decrees
which they had passed to his honor. Vast
crowds had assembled to witness the ceremony
Cæsar was seated in a magnificent chair, which
might have been called either a chair or a throne,

and was surrounded by officers and attendants
When the Senate approached, Cæsar did not
rise to receive them, but remained seated, like
a monarch receiving a deputation of his subjects.　The incident would not seem to be in
itself of any great importance, but, considered
as an indication of Cæsar's designs, it attracted
great attention, and produced a very general excitement.　The act was adroitly managed so
as to be somewhat equivocal in its character, in
order that it might be represented one way or
the other on the following day, according as the
indications of public sentiment might incline.
Some said that Cæsar was intending to rise,
but was prevented, and held down by those who
stood around him.　Others said that an officer
motioned to him to rise, but he rebuked his interference by a frown, and continued his seat.
Thus while, in fact, he received the Roman
Senate as their monarch and sovereign, his own
intentions and designs in so doing were left
somewhat in doubt, in order to avoid awakening
a sudden and violent opposition.

Not long after this, as he was returning in
public from some great festival, the streets being
full of crowds, and the populace following him
in great throngs with loud acclamations, a man

went up to his statue as he passed it, and placed upon the head of it a laurel crown, fastened with a white ribbon, which was a badge of royalty. Some officers ordered the ribbon to be taken down, and sent the man to prison. Cæsar was very much displeased with the officers, and dismissed them from their office. He wished, he said, to have the opportunity to disavow, himself, such claims, and not to have others disavow them for him.

Cæsar's disavowals were, however, so faint, and people had so little confidence in their sincerity, that the cases became more and more frequent in which the titles and symbols of royalty were connected with his name. The people who wished to gain his favor saluted him in public with the name of *Rex*, the Latin word for king. He replied that his name was Cæsar, not *Rex*, showing, however, no other signs of displeasure. On one great occasion, a high public officer, a near relative of his, repeatedly placed a diadem upon his head, Cæsar himself, as often as he did it, gently putting it off. At last he sent the diadem away to a temple that was near, saying that there was no king in Rome but Jupiter. In a word, all his conduct indicated that he wished to have it appear that

the people were pressing the crown upon him,
when he himself was steadily refusing it.

This state of things produced a very strong
and universal, though suppressed excitement in
the city. Parties were formed. Some began
to be willing to make Cæsar king; others were
determined to hazard their lives to prevent it.
None dared, however, openly to utter their sentiments on either side. They expressed them
by mysterious looks and dark intimations. At
the time when Cæsar refused to rise to receive
the Senate, many of the members withdrew in
silence, and with looks of offended dignity
When the crown was placed upon his statue or
upon his own brow, a portion of the populace
would applaud with loud acclamations; and
whenever he disavowed these acts, either by
words or counter-actions of his own, an equally
loud acclamation would arise from the other
side. On the whole, however, the idea that
Cæsar was gradually advancing toward the
kingdom steadily gained ground.

And yet Cæsar himself spoke frequently with
great humility in respect to his pretensions and
claims; and when he found public sentiment
turning against the ambitious schemes he seems
secretly to have cherished, he wou'd present

some excuse or explanation for his conduct plausible enough to answer the purpose of a disa-
vowal.   When he received the Senate, sitting
like a king, on the occasion before referred to,
when they read to him the decrees which they
had passed in his favor, he replied to them that
there was more need of diminishing the public
honors which he received than of increasing
them.   When he found, too, how much excitement his conduct on that occasion had produced,
he explained it by saying that he had retained
his sitting posture on account of the infirmity
of his health, as it made him dizzy to stand.
He thought, probably, that these pretexts would
tend to quiet the strong and turbulent spirits
around him, from whose envy or rivalry he had
most to fear, without at all interfering with the
effect which the act itself would have produced
upon the masses of the population.   He wished,
in a word, to accustom them to see him assume
the position and the bearing of a sovereign,
while, by his apparent humility in his intercourse with those immediately around him, h
avoided as much as possible irritating an l
arousing the jealous and watchful rivals wl
were next to him in power.

If this were his plan, it seemed to he advanc-

ing prosperously toward its accomplishment
The population of the city seemed to become
more and more familiar with the idea that Cæsar
was about to become a king.   The opposition
which the idea had at first awakened appeared
to subside, or, at least, the public expression of
it, which daily became more and more determined and dangerous, was restrained.   At length
the time arrived when it appeared safe to intro-
duce the subject to the Roman Senate.   This,
of course, was a hazardous experiment.   It was
managed, however, in a very adroit and ingeni-
ous manner.

There were in Rome, and, in fact, in many
other cities and countries of the world in those
days, a variety of prophetic books, called the
Sibylline Oracles, in which it was generally believed that future events were foretold.   Some
of these volumes or rolls, which were very ancient and of great authority, were preserved in
the temples at Rome, under the charge of a
board of guardians, who were to keep them with
the utmost care, and to consult them on great
occasions, in order to discover beforehand what
would be the result of public measures or great
enterprises which were in contemplation.   It
happened that at this time the Romans were

B.C. 44.]   THE CONSPIRACY.   245

Declaration of the Sibylline books.   Plan for crowning Cæsar

engaged in a war with the Parthians, a very
wealthy and powerful nation of Asia. Cæsar
was making preparations for an expedition to
the East to attempt to subdue this people. He
gave orders that the Sibylline Oracles should
be consulted. The proper officers, after con-
sulting them with the usual solemn ceremonies,
reported to the Senate that they found it recorded in these sacred prophecies that the Parthians could not be conquered except by a *king*.
A senator proposed, therefore, that, to meet the
emergency, Cæsar should be made king during
the war. There was at first no decisive action
on this proposal. It was dangerous to express
any opinion. People were thoughtful, serious,
and silent, as on the eve of some great convul-
sion. No one knew what others were meditating, and thus did not dare to express his own
wishes or designs. There soon, however, was
a prevailing understanding that Cæsar's friends
were determined on executing the design of
crowning him, and that the fifteenth of March,
called, in their phraseology, the *Ides of March*,
was fixed upon as the coronation day.

In the mean time, Cæsar's enemies, though
to all outward appearance quiet and calm, had
not been inactive. Finding that his plans were

now ripe for execution, and that they had no
open means of resisting them, they formed a
conspiracy to assassinate Cæsar himself, and
thus bring his ambitious schemes to an effectual
and final end.   The name of the original leader
of this conspiracy was Cassius.

Cassius had been for a long time Cæsar's
personal rival and enemy.   He was a man of
a very violent and ardent temperament, impetuous and fearless, very fond of exercising power
himself, but very restless and uneasy in having
it exercised over him.   He had all the Roman
repugnance to being under the authority of a
master, with an additional personal determination of his own not to submit to Cæsar.   He
determined to slay Cæsar rather than to allow
him to be made a king, and he went to work,
with great caution, to bring other leading and
influential men to join him in this determination.   Some of those to whom he applied said
that they would unite with him in his plot provided he would get Marcus Brutus to join them.

Brutus was the prætor of the city.   The
prætorship of the city was a very high municipal office.   The conspirators wished to have
Brutus join them partly on account of his station as a magistrate, as if they supposed that

oy having the highest public magistrate of the city for their leader in the deed, the destruction of their victim would appear less like a murder, and would be invested, instead, in some respects, with the sanctions and with the dignity of an official execution.

Then, again, they wished for the moral support which would be afforded them in their desperate enterprise by Brutus's extraordinary personal character. He was younger than Cassius, but he was grave, thoughtful, taciturn, calm—a man of inflexible integrity, of the coolest determination, and, at the same time, of the most undaunted courage. The conspirators distrusted one another, for the resolution of impetuous men is very apt to fail when the emergency arrives which puts it to the test; but as for Brutus, they knew very well that whatever he undertook he would most certainly do.

There was a great deal even in his name. It was a Brutus that five centuries before had been the main instrument of the expulsion of the Roman kings. He had secretly meditated the design, and, the better to conceal it, had feigned idiocy, as the story was, that he might not be watched or suspected until the favorable hour for executing his design should arrive. He therefore ceased to speak, and seemed to lose his reason; he wandered about the city silent and gloomy, like a brute. His name had been Lucius Junius before. They added Brutus now, to designate his condition. When at last, however, the crisis arrived which he judged favorable for the expulsion of the kings, he suddenly reassumed his speech and his reason, called the astonished Romans to arms, and triumphantly accomplished his design. His name and memory had been cherished ever since that day as of a great deliverer.

They, therefore, who looked upon Cæsar as another king, naturally turned their thoughts to the Brutus of their day, hoping to find in him another deliverer. Brutus found, from time to time, inscriptions on his ancient namesake's statue expressing the wish that he were now alive. He also found each morning, as he came to the tribunal where he was accustomed to sit in the discharge of the duties of his office, brief writings, which had been left there during the night, in which few words expressed deep meaning, such as "Awake, Brutus, to thy duty;" and "Art thou indeed a Brutus?"

Still it seemed hardly probable that Brutus could be led to take a decided stand against

Cæsar, for they had been warm personal friends ever since the conclusion of the civil wars. Brutus had, indeed, been on Pompey's side while that general lived; he fought with him at the battle of Pharsalia, but he had been taken prisoner there, and Cæsar, instead of executing him as a traitor, as most victorious generals in a civil war would have done, spared his life, forgave him for his hostility, received him into his own service, and afterward raised him to very high and honorable stations. He gave him the government of the richest province, and, after his return from it, loaded with wealth and honors, he made him prætor of the city. In a word, it would seem that he had done every thing which it was possible to do to make him one of his most trustworthy and devoted friends. The men, therefore, to whom Cassius first applied, perhaps thought that they were very safe in saying that they would unite in the intended conspiracy if he would get Brutus to join them.

They expected Cassius himself to make the attempt to secure the co-operation of Brutus, as Cassius was on terms of intimacy with him on account of a family connection. Cassius's wife was the sister of Brutus. This had made the two men intimate associates and warm friends

in former years, though they had been recently
somewhat estranged from each other on account
of having been competitors for the same offices
and honors. In these contests Cæsar had decided in favor of Brutus. "Cassius," said he,
on one such occasion, " gives the best reasons ;
but I can not refuse Brutus any thing he asks
for."   In fact, Cæsar had conceived a strong
personal friendship for Brutus, and believed him
to be entirely devoted to his cause.

Cassius, however, sought an interview with
Brutus, with a view of engaging him in his design.   He easily effected his own reconciliation
with him, as he had himself been the offended
party in their estrangement from each other.
He asked Brutus whether he intended to be
present in the Senate on the Ides of March,
when the friends of Cæsar, as was understood,
were intending to present him with the crown.
Brutus said he should not be there.   " But suppose," said Cassius, " we are specially sum
moned."   " Then," said Brutus, " I shall go,
and shall be ready to die if necessary to defend
the liberty of my country."

Cassius then assured Brutus that there were
many other Roman citizens, of the highest rank,
who were animated by the same determination.

and that they all looked up to him to lead and
direct them in the work which it was now very
evident must be done.   "Men look," said Cassius, "to other prætors to entertain them with
games, spectacles, and shows, but they have
very different ideas in respect to you.   Your
character, your name, your position, your an-
cestry, and the course of conduct which you
have already always pursued, inspire the whole
city with the hope that you are to be their deliverer.   The citizens are all ready to aid you,
and to sustain you at the hazard of their lives;
but they look to you to go forward, and to act
in their name and in their behalf, in the crisis
which is now approaching."

Men of a very calm exterior are often sus-
ceptible of the profoundest agitations within,
the emotions seeming to be sometimes all the
more permanent and uncontrollable from the
absence of outward display.   Brutus said little,
but his soul was excited and fired by Cassius's
words.   There was a struggle in his soul between his grateful sense of his political obligations to Cæsar and his personal attachment to
him on the one hand, and, on the other, a certain stern Roman conviction that every thing
should be sacrificed, even friendship and grati-

tude, as well as fortune and life, to the welfare
of his country.   He acceded to the plan, and
began forthwith to enter upon the necessary
measures for putting it into execution.

There was a certain general, named Ligurius, who had been in Pompey's army, and
whose hostility to Cæsar had never been really
subdued.   He was now sick.   Brutus went to
see him.   He found him in his bed.   The excitement in Rome was so intense, though the
expressions of it were suppressed and restrained,
that every one was expecting continually some
great event, and every motion and look was in-
terpreted to have some deep meaning.   Ligurius read in the countenance of Brutus, as he
approached his bedside, that he had not come on
any trifling errand.   "Ligurius," said Brutus,
"this is not a time for *you* to be sick."   "Brutus," replied Ligurius, rising at once from his
couch, "if you have any enterprise in mind that
is worthy of you, I am well."   Brutus explained
to the sick man their design, and he entered into
it with ardor.

The plan was divulged to one after another
of such men as the conspirators supposed most
worthy of confidence in such a desperate undertaking, and meetings for consultation were held

to determine what plan to adopt for finally accomplishing their end. It was agreed that
Cæsar must be slain ; but the time, the place,
and the manner in which the deed should be
performed were all yet undecided. Various
plans were proposed in the consultations which
the conspirators held ; but there was one thing
peculiar to them all, which was, that they did
not any of them contemplate or provide for any
thing like secrecy in the commission of the
deed. It was to be performed in the most open
and public manner. With a stern and undaunted boldness, which has always been considered by mankind as truly sublime, they determined that, in respect to the actual execution
itself of the solemn judgment which they had
pronounced, there should be nothing private or
concealed. They thought over the various public situations in which they might find Cæsar,
and where they might strike him down, only to
select the one which would be most public of
all. They kept, of course, their preliminary
counsels private, to prevent the adoption of
measures for counteracting them ; but they
were to perform the deed in such a manner as
that, so soon as it was performed, they should
stand out to view, exposed fully to the gaze of

all mankind as the authors of it. They planned no retreat, no concealment, no protection whatever for themselves, seeming to feel that the deed which they were about to perform, of destroying the master and monarch of the world, was a deed in its own nature so grand and sublime as to raise the perpetrators of it entirely above all considerations relating to their own personal safety. Their plan, therefore, was to keep their consultations and arrangements secret until they were prepared to strike the blow, then to strike it in the most public and imposing manner possible, and calmly afterward to await the consequences.

In this view of the subject, they decided that the chamber of the Roman Senate was the proper place, and the Ides of March, the day on which he was appointed to be crowned, was the proper time for Cæsar to be slain.

CHAPTER XII.

THE ASSASSINATION.

ACCORDING to the account given by his historians, Cæsar received many warnings of his approaching fate, which, however, he would not heed. Many of these warnings were strange portents and prodigies, which the philosophical writers who recorded them half believed themselves, and which they were always ready to add to their narratives even if they did not believe them, on account of the great influence which such an introduction of the supernatural and the divine had with readers in those days in enhancing the dignity and the dramatic interest of the story. These warnings were as follows:

At Capua, which was a great city at some distance south of Rome, the second, in fact, in Italy, and the one which Hannibal had proposed to make his capital, some workmen were removing certain ancient sepulchers to make room for the foundations of a splendid edifice which, among his other plans for the embellishment of the cities of Italy, Cæsar was intending to have

erected there.   As the excavations advanced,
the workmen came at last to an ancient tomb,
which proved to be that of the original founder
of Capua ; and, in bringing out the sarcophagus,
they found an inscription, worked upon a brass
plate, and in the Greek character, predicting
that if those remains were ever disturbed, a
great member of the Julian family would be
assassinated by his own friends, and his death
would be followed by extended devastations
throughout all Italy.

The horses, too, with which Cæsar had passed
the Rubicon, and which had been, ever since
that time, living in honorable retirement in a
splendid park which Cæsar had provided for
them, by some mysterious instinct, or from
some divine communication, had warning of the
approach of their great benefactor's end.   They
refused their food, and walked about with melancholy and dejected looks, mourning apparently,
and in a manner almost human, some impending grief.

There was a class of prophets in those days
called by a name which has been translated
soothsayers.   These soothsayers were able, as
was supposed, to look somewhat into futurity—
dimly and doubtfully, it is true, but really, by

means of certain appearances exhibited by the
bodies of the animals offered in sacrifices
These soothsayers were consulted on all important occasions; and if the auspices proved
unfavorable when any great enterprise was
about to be undertaken, it was often, on that
account, abandoned or postponed. One of these
soothsayers, named Spurinna, came to Cæsar
one day, and informed him that he had found,
by means of a public sacrifice which he had just
been offering, that there was a great and mysterious danger impending over him, which was
connected in some way with the Ides of March,
and he counseled him to be particularly cautious
and circumspect until that day should have
passed.

The Senate were to meet on the Ides of
March in a new and splendid edifice, which had
been erected for their use by Pompey. There
was in the interior of the building, among other
decorations, a statue of Pompey. The day before the Ides of March, some birds of prey from
a neighboring grove came flying into this hall,
pursuing a little wren with a sprig of laurel in
its mouth. The birds tore the wren to pieces,
the laurel dropping from its bill to the marble
pavement of the floor below. Now, as Cæsar

31—17

had been always accustomed to wear a crown
of laurel on great occasions, and had always
evinced a particular fondness for that decoration,
that plant had come to be considered his own
proper badge, and the fall of the laurel, therefore, was naturally thought to portend some
great calamity to him.

The night before the Ides of March Cæsar
could not sleep. It would not seem, however,
to be necessary to suppose any thing supernatural to account for his wakefulness. He lay
upon his bed restless and excited, or if he fell
into a momentary slumber, his thoughts, instead of finding repose, were only plunged into
greater agitations, produced by strange, and, as
he thought, supernatural dreams. He imagined
that he ascended into the skies, and was received
there by Jupiter, the supreme divinity, as an
associate and equal. While shaking hands with
the great father of gods and men, the sleeper
was startled by a frightful sound. He awoke,
and found his wife Calpurnia groaning and
struggling in her sleep. He saw her by the
moonlight which was shining into the room.
He spoke to her, and aroused her. After staring
wildly for a moment till she had recovered her
thoughts, she said that she had had a dreadful

dream. She had dreamed that the roof of the house had fallen in, and that, at the same instant, the doors had been burst open, and some robber or assassin had stabbed her husband as he was lying in her arms. The philosophy of those days found in these dreams mysterious and preternatural warnings of impending danger; that of ours, however, sees nothing either in the absurd sacrilegiousness of Cæsar's thoughts, or his wife's incoherent and inconsistent images of terror — nothing more than the natural and proper effects, on the one hand, of the insatiable ambition of man, and, on the other, of the conjugal affection and solicitude of woman. The ancient sculptors carved out images of men, by the forms and lineaments of which we see that the physical characteristics of humanity have not changed. History seems to do the same with the affections and passions of the soul. The dreams of Cæsar and his wife on the night before the Ides of March, as thus recorded, form a sort of spiritual statue, which remains from generation to generation, to show us how precisely all the inward workings of human nature are from age to age the same.

When the morning came Cæsar and Calpurnia arose, both restless and ill at ease. Cæsar

ordered the auspices to be consulted with refer
ence to the intended proceedings of the day.
The soothsayers came in in due time, and reported that the result was unfavorable.   Calpurnia, too, earnestly entreated her husband not
to go to the senate-house that day.   She had
a very strong presentiment that, if he did go,
some great calamity would ensue.   Cæsar himself hesitated.   He was half inclined to yield,
and postpone his coronation to another occasion.

In the course of the day, while Cæsar was in
this state of doubt and uncertainty, one of the
conspirators, named Decimus Brutus, came in.
This Brutus was not a man of any extraordinary courage or energy, but he had been invited
by the other conspirators to join them, on ac
count of his having under his charge a large
number of gladiators, who, being desperate and
reckless men, would constitute a very suitable
armed force for them to call in to their aid in
case of any emergency arising which should require it.

The conspirators having thus all their plans
arranged, Decimus Brutus was commissioned
to call at Cæsar's house when the time approached for the assembling of the Senate, both
'o avert suspicion from Cæsar's mind, and to

assure himself that nothing had been discovered
It was in the afternoon, the time for the meeting of the senators having been fixed at five
o'clock.   Decimus Brutus found Cæsar troubled
and perplexed, and uncertain what to do.   After
hearing what he had to say, he replied by urg
ing him to go by all means to the senate-house,
as he had intended.   " You have formally called
the Senate together," said he, " and they are
now assembling.   They are all prepared to con-
fer upon you the rank and title of king, not only
in Parthia, while you are conducting this war
but every where, by sea and land, except in
Italy.   And now, while they are all in their
places, waiting to consummate the great act,
how absurd will it be for you to send them word
to go home again, and come back some other
day, when Calpurnia shall have had better
dreams !"

He urged, too, that, even if Cæsar was determined to put off the action of the Senate to
another day, he was imperiously bound to go
himself and adjourn the session in person.   So
saying, he took the hesitating potentate by the
arm, and adding to his arguments a little gen
tle force, conducted him along.

The conspirators supposed that all was safe

The fact was, however, that all had been discovered.　There was a certain Greek, a teacher
of oratory, named Artemidorus.　He had contrived to learn something of the plot from some
of the conspirators who were his pupils.　He
wrote a brief statement of the leading particulars, and, having no other mode of access to
Cæsar, he determined to hand it to him on the
way as he went to the senate-house.　Of course,
the occasion was one of great public interest,
and crowds had assembled in the streets to see
the great conqueror as he went along.　As
usual at such times, when powerful officers of
state appear in public, many people came up
to present petitions to him as he passed.　These
he received, and handed them, without reading,
to his secretary who attended him, as if to have
them preserved for future examination.　Artemidorus, who was waiting for his opportunity,
when he perceived what disposition Cæsar made
of the papers which were given to him, began
to be afraid that his own communication would
not be attended to until it was too late.　He
accordingly pressed up near to Cæsar, refusing
to allow any one else to pass the paper in; and
when, at last, he obtained an opportunity, he
gave it directly into Cæsar's hands, saying to

him, "Read this immediately: it concerns your-
self, and is of the utmost importance"

Cæsar took the paper and attempted to read
it, but new petitions and other interruptions
constantly prevented him; finally he gave up
the attempt, and went on his way, receiving and
passing to his secretary all other papers, but retaining this paper of Artemidorus in his hand.

Cæsar passed Spurinna on his way to the
senate-house—the soothsayer who had predict-
ed some great danger connected with the Ides
of March. As soon as he recognized him, he
accosted him with the words, "Well, Spurinna,
the Ides of March have come, and I am safe."
"Yes," replied Spurinna, "they have come, but
they are not yet over."

At length he arrived at the senate-house, with
the paper of Artemidorus still unread in his
hand. The senators were all convened, the
leading conspirators among them. They all
rose to receive Cæsar as he entered. Cæsar
advanced to the seat provided for him, and, when
he was seated, the senators themselves sat down
The moment had now arrived, and the conspirators, with pale looks and beating hearts, felt
that now or never the deed was to be done.

It requires a very considerable degree of phys-

ıcal courage and hardihood for men to come to
a calm and deliberate decision that they wil
kill one whom they hate, and, still more, actually to strike the blow, even when under the
immediate impulse of passion. But men who
are perfectly capable of either of these often find
their resolution fail them as the time comes for
striking a dagger into the living flesh of their
victim, when he sits at ease and unconcerned
before them, unarmed and defenseless, and doing
nothing to excite those feelings of irritation and
anger which are generally found so necessary to
nerve the human arm to such deeds.   Utter de-
fenselessness is accordingly, sometimes, a greater protection than an armor of steel.

Even Cassius himself, the originator and the
soul of the whole enterprise, found his courage
hardly adequate to the work now that the moment had arrived ; and, in order to arouse the
necessary excitement in his soul, he looked up
to the statue of Pompey, Cæsar's ancient and
most formidable enemy, and invoked its aid.
It gave him its aid.   It inspired him with some
portion of the enmity with which the soul of
its great original had burned ; and thus the sou.
of the living assassin was nerved to its work by
a sort of sympathy with a block of stone.

Foreseeing the necessity of something like a stimulus to action when the immediate moment for action should arrive, the conspirators had agreed that, as soon as Cæsar was seated, they would approach him with a petition, which he would probably refuse, and then, gathering around him, they would urge him with their importunities, so as to produce, in the confusion, a sort of excitement that would make it easier for them to strike the blow.

There was one person, a relative and friend of Cæsar's, named Marcus Antonius, called commonly, however, in English narratives, Marc Antony, the same who has been already mentioned as having been subsequently connected with Cleopatra. He was a very energetic and determined man, who, they thought, might possibly attempt to defend him. To prevent this, one of the conspirators had been designated to take him aside, and occupy his attention with some pretended subject of discourse, ready, at the same time, to resist and prevent his interference if he should show himself inclined to offer any.

Things being thus arranged, the petitioner, as had been agreed, advanced to Cæsar with his petition, others coming up at the same time as if to second the request. The object of the petition was to ask for the pardon of the brother of one of the conspirators. Cæsar declined granting it. The others then crowded around him, urging him to grant the request with pressing importunities, all apparently reluctant to strike the first blow. Cæsar began to be alarmed, and attempted to repel them. One of them then pulled down his robe from his neck to lay it bare. Cæsar arose, exclaiming, "But this is violence." At the same instant, one of the conspirators struck at him with his sword, and wounded him slightly in the neck.

All was now terror, outcry, and confusion. Cæsar had no time to draw his sword, but fought a moment with his style, a sharp instrument of iron with which they wrote, in those days, on waxen tablets, and which he happened then to have in his hand. With this instrument he ran one of his enemies through the arm.

This resistance was just what was necessary to excite the conspirators, and give them the requisite resolution to finish their work. Cæsar soon saw the swords, accordingly, gleaming all around him, and thrusting themselves at him on every side. The senators rose in confusion

and dismay, perfectly thunderstruck at the
scene, and not knowing what to do. Antony
perceived that all resistance on his part would
be unavailing, and accordingly did not attempt
any. Cæsar defended himself alone for a few
minutes as well as he could, looking all around
him in vain for help, and retreating at the same
time toward the pedestal of Pompey's statue.
At length, when he saw Brutus among his murderers, he exclaimed, "And you too, Brutus?"
and seemed from that moment to give up in
despair. He drew his robe over his face, and

POMPEY'S STATUE.

soon fell under the wounds which he received.
His blood ran out upon the pavement at the
foot of Pompey's statue, as if his death were a
sacrifice offered to appease his ancient enemy's
revenge.

In the midst of the scene Brutus made an
attempt to address the senators, and to vindicate what they had done, but the confusion and
excitement were so great that it was impossible
that any thing could be heard. The senators
were, in fact, rapidly leaving the place, going
off in every direction, and spreading the tidings
over the city. The event, of course, produced
universal commotion. The citizens began to
close their shops, and some to barricade their
houses, while others hurried to and fro about the
streets, anxiously inquiring for intelligence, and
wondering what dreadful event was next to
be expected. Antony and Lepidus, who were
Cæsar's two most faithful and influential friends,
not knowing how extensive the conspiracy might
be, nor how far the hostility to Cæsar and his
party might extend, fled, and, not daring to go
to their own houses, lest the assassins or their
confederates might pursue them there, sought
concealment in the houses of friends on whom
they supposed they could rely and who were
willing to receive them.

In the mean time, the conspirators, glorying in the deed which they had perpetrated, and congratulating each other on the successful issue of their enterprise, sallied forth together from the senate-house, leaving the body of their victim weltering in its blood, and marched, with drawn swords in their hands, along the streets from the senate-house to the Capitol. Brutus went at the head of them, preceded by a liberty cap borne upon the point of a spear, and with his bloody dagger in his hand. The Capitol was the citadel, built magnificently upon the Capitoline Hill, and surrounded by temples, and other sacred and civil edifices, which made the spot the architectural wonder of the world. As Brutus and his company proceeded thither, they announced to the citizens, as they went along, the great deed of deliverance which they had wrought out for the country. Instead of seeking concealment, they gloried in the work which they had done, and they so far succeeded in inspiring others with a portion of their enthusiasm, that some men who had really taken no part in the deed joined Brutus and his company in their march, to obtain by stealth a share in the glory.

The body of Cæsar lay for some time un-

heeded where it had fallen, the attention of
every one being turned to the excitement, which
was extending through the city, and to the ex
pectation of other great events which might suddenly develop themselves in other quarters of
Rome.   There were left only three of Cæsar's
slaves, who gathered around the body to look at
the wounds.   They counted them, and found
the number twenty-three.   It shows, however,
how strikingly, and with what reluctance, the
actors in this tragedy came up to their work at
last, that of all these twenty-three wounds only
one was a mortal one.   In fact, it is probable
that, while all of the conspirators struck the
victim in their turn, to fulfill the pledge which
they had given to one another that they would
every one inflict a wound, each one hoped that
the fatal blow would be given, after all, by some
other hand than his own.

At last the slaves decided to convey the
body home.   They obtained a sort of chair,
which was made to be borne by poles, and
placed the body upon it.   Then, lifting at the
three handles, and allowing the fourth to hang
unsupported for want of a man, they bore the
ghastly remains home to the distracted Calpurnia.

The next day Brutus and his associates called
an assembly of the people in the Forum, and
made an address to them, explaining the mo-
tives which had led them to the commission of
the deed, and vindicating the necessity and the
justice of it. The people received these expla-
nations in silence. They expressed neither approbation nor displeasure. It was not, in fact,
to be expected that they would feel or evince
any satisfaction at the loss of their master. He
had been their champion, and, as they believed,
their friend. The removal of Cæsar brought
no accession of power nor increase of liberty to
them. It might have been a gain to ambitious
senators, or powerful generals, or high officers
of state, by removing a successful rival out of
their way, but it seemed to promise little advantage to the community at large, other than
the changing of one despotism for another. Besides, a populace who know that they must be
governed, prefer generally, if they must submit to some control, to yield their submission
to some one master spirit whom they can ook
up to as a great and acknowledged superior.
They had rather have a Cæsar than a Senate
to command them.

The higher authorities, however, were, as

might have been expected, disposed to acqui-
esce in the removal of Cæsar from his intended
throne.   The Senate met, and passed an act of
indemnity, to shield the conspirators from all
legal liability for the deed they had done.   In
order, however, to satisfy the people too, as far
as possible, they decreed divine honors to Cæsar,
confirmed and ratified all that he had done while
in the exercise of supreme power, and appointed
a time for the funeral, ordering arrangements
to be made for a very pompous celebration of it

A will was soon found, which Cæsar, it seems,
had made some time before.   Calpurnia's father
proposed that this will should be opened and
read in public at Antony's house; and this was
accordingly done.   The provisions of the will
were, many of them, of such a character as renewed the feelings of interest and sympathy
which the people of Rome had begun to cherish
for Cæsar's memory.   His vast estate was divided chiefly among the children of his sister,
as he had no children of his own, while the
very men who had been most prominent in
his assassination were named as trustees and
guardians of the property; and one of them,
Decimus Brutus, the one who had been so ur-
gent to conduct him to the senate-house, was a

second heir.　He had some splendid gardens near the Tiber, which he bequeathed to the citizens of Rome, and a large amount of money also, to be divided among them, sufficient to give every man a considerable sum.

The time for the celebration of the funeral ceremonies was made known by proclamation, and, as the concourse of strangers and citizens of Rome was likely to be so great as to forbid the forming of all into one procession without consuming more than one day, the various classes of the community were invited to come, each in their own way, to the Field of Mars, bringing with them such insignia, offerings, and oblations as they pleased.　The Field of Mars was an immense parade ground, reserved for military reviews, spectacles, and shows.　A funeral pile was erected here for the burning of the body There was to be a funeral discourse pronounced, and Marc Antony had been designated to perform this duty.　The body had been placed in a gilded bed, under a magnificent canopy in the form of a temple, before the rostra where the funeral discourse was to be pronounced.　The bed was covered with scarlet and cloth of gold and at the head of it was laid the robe in which Cæsar had been slain.　It was stained with

blood, and pierced with the holes that the swords
and daggers of the conspirators had made.

Marc Antony, instead of pronouncing a for
mal panegyric upon his deceased friend, ordered
a crier to read the decrees of the Senate, in
which all honors, human and divine, had been
ascribed to Cæsar.   He then added a few words
of his own.   The bed was then taken up, with
the body upon it, and borne out into the Forum,
preparatory to conveying it to the pile which
had been prepared for it upon the Field of Mars.
A question, however, here arose among the
multitude assembled in respect to the proper
place for burning the body.   The people seemed
inclined to select the most honorable place which
could be found within the limits of the city.
Some proposed a beautiful temple on the Capitoline Hill.   Others wished to take it to the
senate-house, where he had been slain.   The
Senate, and those who were less inclined to pay
extravagant honors to the departed hero, were
in favor of some more retired spot, under pre
tense that the buildings of the city would be en
dangered by the fire.   This discussion was fast
becoming a dispute, when it was suddenly ended
by two men, with swords at their sides and
lances in their hands, forcing their way through

BURNING OF CÆSAR'S BODY.

the crowd with lignted torches, and setting the
bed and its canopy on fire where it lay.

This settled the question, and the whole company were soon in the wildest excitement with
the work of building up a funeral pile upon the
spot. At first they brought fagots and threw
upon the fire, then benches from the neighboring courts and porticoes, and then any thing
combustible which came to hand. The honor
done to the memory of a deceased hero was, in
some sense, in proportion to the greatness of his
funeral pile, and all the populace on this occasion began soon to seize every thing they
could find, appropriate and unappropriate, provided that it would increase the flame. The
soldiers threw on their lances and spears, the
musicians their instruments, and others stripped
off the cloths and trappings from the furniture
of the procession, and heaped them upon the
burning pile.

So fierce and extensive was the fire, that it
spread to some of the neighboring houses, and
required great efforts to prevent a general con-
flagration. The people, too, became greatly ex
cited by the scene. They lighted torches by the
fire, and went to the houses of Brutus and Cassius, threatening vengeance upon them for the

murder of Cæsar. The authorities succeeded
though with infinite difficulty, in protecting
Brutus and Cassius from the violence of the
mob, but they seized one unfortunate citizer
of the name of Cinna, thinking it a certain
Cinna who had been known as an enemy of
Cæsar. They cut off his head, notwithstanding
his shrieks and cries, and carried it about the
city on the tip of a pike, a dreadful symbol of
their hostility to the enemies of Cæsar. As
frequently happens, however, in such deeds of
sudden violence these hasty and lawless aven-
gers found afterward that they had made a
mistake, and beheaded the wrong man.

The Roman people erected a column to the
memory of Cæsar, on which they placed the inscription, "To the Father of his Country."
They fixed the figure of a star upon the summit
of it, and some time afterward, while the people
were celebrating some games in honor of his
memory, a great comet blazed for seven nights
in the sky, which they recognized as the mighty
hero's soul reposing in heaven.

THE END.